PROJECT ENGINEER: Lyman Coleman, Serendipity House

WRITER FOR NOTES/COMMENTARY: Richard Peace, Gordon Conwell Seminary.

CONTRIBUTORS: Denny Rydberg, University Presbyterian Church, Seattle □ Gordon Fee, Gordon Conwell Seminary, Boston □ Virginia Zachert, Medical College of Georgia, Augusta □ Margaret Coleman, Serendipity House, Denver □ Peter Menconi, Professional Consultants, Denver □ John Mallison, Board of Education, Uniting Church in Australia, Sydney □ John U'Ren, Scripture Union, Melbourne □ Ken Anderson, Synod of South Australia, Uniting Church of Australia, Adelaide □ Anton Baumohl, Scripture Union, Bristol, England □ Lance Pierson, Freelance writer, London □ Emlyn Williams, Scripture Union, Cambridge, England.

PUBLISHER: Serendipity House is a resource community specializing in the equipping of pastors and church leaders for small group ministry in the local church in the English speaking world. A list of training events and resources can be obtained by writing one of the addresses below.

SERENDIPITY U.S.A.
Serendipity House
Box 1012
Littleton, Colorado 80160

Telephone: 800-525-9563

SERENDIPITY AUSTRALIA
Serendipity Christian Resources
P.O. Box 130
West Ryde, NSW 2114

Telephone: SYDNEY 858-1778

SERENDIPITY GREAT BRITAIN
c/o Serendipity U.K.
48 Peterborough Road
London SW6 3EB

Telephone: LONDON 01-731-6544

94 95 96 97 98 / CHG / 8 7 6 5 4 3 2

1 JOHN

LYMAN COLEMAN and RICHARD PEACE

This Book is the Property of

Countryside Christian Church

Mission, Kansas

MASTERING THE BASICS

PERSONAL EXCELLENCE THROUGH BIBLE STUDY

Mastering The Basics

PERSONAL EXCELLENCE THROUGH BIBLE STUDY

All Scripture is God-breathed
and is useful for teaching,
rebuking, correcting
and training in righteousness,
so that the man of God
may be thoroughly equipped
for every good work.

2 TIMOTHY 3:16-17 NIV

THREE PARTS TO THE PROGRAM: CHOOSE ONE, TWO, OR ALL THREE

Some like to travel alone. Some like to travel in groups. Some like to travel with a small group on a huge passenger liner with a tour guide and lectures along the way.

In this program you can do all three: (1) Self study—on your own, (2) Group study—with a small intimate group, or (3) Church-wide groups—with the pastor or associate minister providing exegetical teaching on the passage when all of the groups get together.

1.Self Study

Those who cannot be in a group can still do the home assigment and get in on the pastoral teaching of the Scripture passage after having completed the assignment, like a college course.

The Bible study assignment worksheets in this book are designed for lay-people who are beginners at Bible study. The study is inductive—that is, you do your own research and draw your own conclusions. If you don't know the meaning of key words, there is a glossary of terms and a running commentary on the page after the worksheet. The Scripture passage for study is printed next to the worksheet, so that you have all of the material you need to complete the study on your own. Each unit of study will take about 30 to 45 minutes to complete, or about 10 minutes a day.

There are three parts to each worksheet: (1) Read—to get the "bird's eye view" of the passage and jot down your first impressions, (2) Search—to get the "worm's eye view" of the passage—digging into the passage verse by verse with specific questions to look for and jot down, and (3) Apply—to find out what God is saying to you through this Scripture, using a different approach each time—self inventory, written prayer, goal setting, scripture memory,

spiritual principles, practical project, etc.

The self study assignment is coordinated with the group study and the expository teaching from the pastor/teacher, giving you the option of supplementing your spiritual diet with two more forms of Bible study.

2.Group Study

The group approach is not only more fun, but also offers a far greater potential for interaction with the Scripture.

The group can be anything from 3 or 4 people, to 30 or 40 people meeting around card tables in the same house. By dividing into groups of 4, you allow not only for maximum participation, but also make room for new people to join the group without making the group too large for sharing.

The group can meet anytime, anywhere during the week: ☐ in homes ☐ offices ☐ restaurants ☐ at breakfast ☐ over coffee ☐ in the evening ☐ at the Sunday school hour just before the teaching session by the pastor/teacher.

The completed home study assignment becomes the basis for the group sharing experience. On the worksheet for each unit is a "Group Agenda" column with guided questions on three levels of sharing: (1) To Begin/10 Minutes, (2) To Go Deeper/20 Minutes, and (3) To Close/5 to 20 Minutes.

You can either have a trained leader for the group, or rotate the leadership around the group—each person taking the responsibility in turn. If you have more than 5 or 6 in the group and you divide into groups of 4 for sharing, you ask one person in each group to be the leader of the foursome. The leader

5

3.Expository Teaching for All Groups Together

This is the Queen Elizabeth II model—a luxury liner cruise with the whole church on board, and the pastor or associate offering in-depth teaching on the passage after the groups have met.

The teaching session can be open to anyone. In fact, a good way to get people interested in the Self Study and Group Study parts of the program is to start teaching the course at a popular church activity and invite groups to get together and join in.

The Pastor/Teacher Commentary corresponds unit by unit with the Self Study/Group Study Book, with suggestions on how to link what the student has studied and the group has discussed with the teaching session.

Further instructions are provided in the Pastor/Teacher Commentary.

simply looks over the questions in the "Group Agenda" column and chooses questions from the list for sharing.

In the Apply part of Unit One, the group is asked to discuss personal and corporate goals for the time together and agree on a common discipline: (1) to complete the Bible study home assignment before the group meets, (2) to attend the group meetings except in case of emergency, (3) to share in leading the group, (4) to keep anything that is shared in the group in confidence, (5) to reach out to others who are not in a group and invite them to fill the "empty chair", and (6) to attend the teaching session with the Pastor/Teacher.

The group lasts as long as the course lasts. If the group wishes to continue after the course is over, the group will have to decide on another course to study or come up with its own purpose and agenda.

Group Agenda

do?

Divide into groups of 4 before starting on these questions. Follow the time recommendations.

TO BEGIN/10 Minutes (Choose 1 or 2)

☐ Have you ever been to a Jewish bar mitzvah or wedding? ☐ How valuable was your own religious instruction in bringing you to Christ? ☐ What would you do differently about religious instruction for your kids? ☐ What did you jot down for READ? ☐ Who does Paul remind you of in this passage: a prosecuting attorney? a diplomat, a drill sergeant in the Marine Corps, etc.

TO GO DEEPER/20 Minutes (Choose 2 or 3)

☐ Go around and answer the questions under SEARCH—one person answering question 1, the next person answering 2, etc. ☐ What's so radical about Paul's teaching here? ☐ Why was Paul so concerned about a minor thing like circumcision? ☐ What would Paul have to say about our Christian rituals and initiation rites today? ☐ Case History: Bob's grandfather was a country preacher; his father was a deacon; and Bob has been on the board of the church for twenty years. "If anybody deserves to go to heaven, it is Bob." Do you agree?

TO CLOSE/5-20 Minutes (Choose 1 or 2)

QUESTIONS

About the Self Study

1. *What if you don't know anything about the Bible?* No problem. The home assignment worksheet is designed to lead you step by step in your study. And, there are Notes on the following page to give you help with key words, places and difficult passages.

2. *What do you mean by the inductive method of Bible study?* It is the scientific method applied to Bible study. You begin by observing facts and draw conclusions based on these facts, just like a scientific experiment.

3. *Why go to all of the trouble of doing your own study if you can find out what the passage really means when the pastor/teacher teaches it on Sunday?* There is no substitute for your own study. None.

About the Group Study

1. *How many do you need to start a group?* Four people, plus an empty chair.

2. *What is the "empty chair" for?* A reminder that there is always room for one more.

3. *What do you do when the group gets too large?* When the group reaches 8, you split into two groups of 4—4 at the kitchen table, and 4 at the dining table. When you reach 12, you add another card table, etc.

4. *What if you have someone in the group who likes to talk (too much)?* On the home assignment worksheet, there is a "Group Agenda" with questions for three levels of sharing: (a) to begin the session, (b) to go deeper, and (c) to close . . . with time limits for each phase. The questions will keep you on track if you follow them.

5. *Who is the leader?* In the first two or three sessions, someone who has been trained by the pastor. After that, you rotate the leadership around the group.

6. *Can you share a book with your wife?* No.

7. *If you run into a conflict that makes it impossible to attend the group meetings, can you stay in the self study part and attend the expository teaching session with the pastor?* Yes.

8. *What if you do not complete the home assignment before the group meeting?* You should still go to the group meeting. In fact, some groups have found it valuable to do their homework together after they get to the meeting.

About the Church-wide Teaching Session

1. *What if the pastor cannot possibly take on the teaching responsibility?* The pastor must be totally committed to this program for it to have maximum impact. If the pastor cannot do the teaching, the pastor should appoint someone else with teaching skills and considerable background in Scripture to do the teaching.

2. *Can people who are not in the self study or group study phases of this program still get in on the teaching session?* Yes.

3. *Can the teaching session be at the Sunday school hour or even the Sunday morning worship service?* Yes. In fact, this would be a good way to interest people in joining a group.

4. *Can the group study and the teaching session be at the same time?* Yes. In fact, this would be a great idea if you have the time and space for groups.

5. *Do you recommend a steady diet of this program?* No. You should take a vacation between courses and disband the groups. Then, when you start a new course, invite the groups to shuffle and reach out to new people.

INTRODUCTION TO THE BOOK OF 1 JOHN

John was an old man when he wrote his first epistle. All the other disciples were dead. Only he remained of the original Twelve. His long life had afforded him the opportunity to witness the spectacular growth of the church. It had begun with only a handful of disciples clustered together in Jerusalem. Now it had spread throughout the known world and the believers had become so numerous that it was difficult to number them all.

But not all that John had seen was good. As well as growth, there had been dissention, defection, and heresy—even in the churches John pastored. In fact, this is why he came to write this epistle: a group of people from his church had gotten involved in strange doctrine. They had then left the church and formed their own community. Now they were trying to persuade other Christians to do the same thing—to leave and join this new group.

So John was compelled to write this letter. In fact, it was an urgent need. Soon, like the other apostles, his time would be at an end. And when he was gone, who would ensure that the church remained loyal to the teachings of Jesus? It was vital that the church understand clearly what lay at the heart of Christianity. It was vital that Christians grasp firmly the nature of the gospel.

So John wrote his first epistle. In it one gets the sense that here John is boiling down the gospel to its essence: "God is light; God is love; Jesus is the Messiah, the Son of God who has come in the flesh; and we are to be his children who have eternal life, who do not continue in sin, and who love one another." This is what it is all about. This is what God has been trying to teach the human race for all these hundreds of years. Here John is distilling all the wisdom and insight of his long years into a few incisive chapters. In the First Epistle of John, therefore, what we have is essential Christianity as seen by the last of the twelve.

John records his final thoughts on the nature of the faith so that, once and for all, we would get it straight. As such, John's epistle is the summation of revelation history and thus it is a book to master—with both heart and head.

Occasion

There were problems in John's church—deep ones that compelled him to write. It is difficult, of course, to reconstruct with full accuracy just what the situation was in the multiple house churches in the Ephesus area where John ministered. Still, it appears that what happened was that a group of Christians got involved in false teaching, split off from the church (2:19), and then started hassling their former friends, probably trying to convince them to espouse their new "advanced" religious views (2:26). (This is a typical response. If you can get others to agree with your newly embraced viewpoint, then you yourself feel more confident that you are, indeed, "right.") Thus John writes this epistle to refute these erroneous views and to encourage those in the church to remain faithful to the gospel as taught by the apostles.

The error of these secessionists was two-fold: (1) they had a defective view of Jesus and (2) a wrong view of sin. On their view of Jesus, they were so caught up with the idea of Jesus as the divine, preexistent Lord that they almost totally neglected his human side. While they probably would not deny that Jesus was a man, to them this fact was insignificant. His humanity did not really matter in comparison to his divinity. As a result they did not believe Jesus to be the Messiah (2:22; 5:1). In particular, they denied that Jesus, as the Son of God, had died. This was the fatal error because it undercut the very heart of the gospel. The gospel defines God as love and love as the laying down of one's life (John 15:13). If Jesus Christ, the Son of God, did not lay down his life for us, then the love of God was not revealed in

Christ. (See the "Comment" on page 14).

They also had an erroneous view of ethics. Specifically, they claimed to be free from sin ... and free from the commandment to love others. Since they did not confess that Jesus was the Messiah, they did not feel any need to obey what he said. And since they felt that they were free from sin, they did not need the Son of God to die in their place for their sins.

These secessionists had come to think of themselves as sort of spiritual "elite," claiming (probably by direct revelation—see 4:1-6) that they had a "deeper" understanding of Christianity than others. As an antidote to this sort of spiritual pride, John reminds his readers again and again that Christians are called upon to love one another. They are not to look down on those brothers and sisters who do not measure up to their own (supposed) superior insight.

It is not clear what, if any, "label" can be affixed to this group of secessionists. The ideas they held were probably related to what later became Gnosticism—a philosophy that taught that matter (including the body) was impure and that "spirit" was all that really counted. Therefore it is not surprising that these secessionists, with this incipient-gnostic view of reality, minimized the humanity of Jesus. To them salvation came via illumination. Thus esoteric "knowledge" is what they sought instead of hearing and heeding apostolic doctrine.

Authorship

But did the apostle John actually write this epistle? This has been the assumption thus far in these notes. Yet there are those scholars who would question whether this is so.

In fact, the author of this letter is nowhere named in 1 John. So, whatever one concludes, it is by way of speculation. However, a good case can be made that John, the beloved apostle, is indeed the author of this epistle. There are a number of reasons for attributing this anonymous epistle to him, including:

1. The strong tradition dating back to the early days of the Church that John was the author.
2. The many similarities in style and content between the Gospel of John and this epistle. The same sharp contrasts appear in both—between light and darkness; truth and falsehood; love and hate. What differences do exist between the two books can be traced to differences in purpose arising out of differences in audience, since the historical context had shifted between the time of the gospel and the time of this epistle.
3. The internal information in the epistle points to John as the author. For example, the author tells us that he was one of the original eyewitnesses of Jesus (1:1-2). Also, the author writes with the air of authority that would be expected of one who was an apostle (see 4:6).

Date

It is very difficult to fix a date to this epistle. The evidence is not clear nor conclusive. However, the best guess is that 1 John was written toward the end of the New Testament era (A.D. 90-95), by which time this gnostic-like heresy had begun to flourish.

Style

1 John is written in the simplest Greek found in all the New Testament. (It is the first book seminary students learn to translate.) 5437 different Greek words appear in the New Testament, yet in the three Johannine epistles, only 303 of these are used—5½ percent of the total. This is not to say, however, that 1 John is a simple, superficial book. On the contrary, it is one of the most profound books in the entire New Testament. Perhaps because of (not

despite) his simple vocabulary John focuses in on the core of the gospel. All else is cut away. He writes only what really matters.

A story is told by Jerome about the "blessed John the evangelist" when he was an extremely old man. According to Jerome, John now has to be carried into the worship service at Ephesus. John is unable to say anything except "little children, love one another," which he repeats over and over. The believers, having heard this same thing so often, ask: "Master, why do you always say this?" "Because," he replied, "it is enough."

Martin Luther wrote: "I have never read a book written in simpler words than this one, and yet the words are inexpressible."

Literary Form

1 John is not an epistle in the sense that 2 and 3 John are (or in the sense of Paul's letters). It does not identify the writer or the recipients. In fact, there is no specific name or place mentioned anywhere in this document. There is no salutation, nor is there a final greeting. It is clear that this is intentional since John knew perfectly well how a letter was written. 3 John has been called by some the most perfect example in the New Testament of Greek letter format. Clearly John was writing a different sort of document.

Three things are evident about John's effort here. First, this is a *literary* document. John states some 13 times that he is *writing* (in contrast to speaking or preaching. See for example 1:4.) Second, it is clear that he has a specific audience in mind which he refers to as "you" (in the plural) some 22 times. Third, there is a so-called "doubled-opening" (similar to that in James) within which John states twice the themes he then develops in the rest of the manuscript. So what we have here is probably a "literary epistle"—a written document addressed to a particular audience. His

audience is the community of churches in and around Ephesus that he pastored and which remained loyal to the gospel he preached.

Outline and Theme

It is difficult to "outline" 1 John—i.e., to track the flow of the author's thought and put it into neat categories and divisions (as one can do with Romans, for example). Rather, it seems that John (much like James) would write a paragraph and then be reminded of a related topic which he would then deal with in the next paragraph. This, in turn, would spark a further thought. This is not to say that John's ideas tumble out in a haphazard fashion. This is certainly not the case. His ideas are focused and interrelated. The ideas hang together—but not by means of a western style of logic. The structure is almost *spiral*, "for the development of a theme often brings us back almost to the starting-point; almost but not quite, for there is a slight shift which provides a transition to a fresh theme; or it may be to a theme which had apparently been dismissed at an earlier point and now comes up for consideration from a slightly different angle." (Dodd)

John's central concern is quite clear, however. He wants to define the marks of a true Christian, over against what was being taught by the secessionists. This is very important. He wants his congregation to have the assurance that they do, indeed, have eternal life (5:13), despite what the false teachers are saying. What, then, are these "marks?" According to John Stott, in 1 John the characteristics of a true Christian are these: right belief (the doctrinal test); righteousness (the moral test); and love (the social test).

Is it possible, therefore, to capture John's exposition in outline form? Not easily! Raymond Brown identifies some 27 different attempts to outline 1 John. Still, it is highly probable that John had some structure in

COMMENTS

mind—even if we are hard-put to reproduce it—since both the Gospel of John and Revelation have coherent outlines. Brown's outline is as follows and is the one that will be used in this book to define the unit divisions[1]:

Outline

I Prologue (1:1-4)

II Part one (1:5—3:10)
- A. The Gospel of God as light; three boasts and three opposite hypotheses (1:5—2:2)
- B. Three claims of intimate knowledge of God to be tested by behavior (2:3-11)
- C. Admonitions to believers: having conquered the Evil One, they must resist the world (2:12-17)
- D. Warning against the secessionists as antichrists who deny the Son and the Father (2:18-27)
- E. God's children versus the Devil's children (2:28—3:10)

III Part Two (3:11—5:21)
- A. The Gospel of loving one another (3:11-24)
- B. The spirits of truth and of deceit, and their respective adherents (4:1-6)
- C. Loving one another as a way of abiding in and loving God (4:7—5:4a)
- D. Faith as conqueror of the world and the role of testimony (5:4b-12)

IV The conclusion (5:13-21)

Further Study

1. Read through 1 John in one sitting. As you do so, list all the characteristics that you can of the false teachers. In another list note down what John defines as the essence of true religion.

[1]pp xx-xxi, *The Epistles of John* (The Anchor Bible), Raymond E. Brown, (Garden City, NY: Doubleday & Company) 1982.

Irenaeus' Second Century Account of the Apostle John

But Polycarp also was not only instructed by apostles, and conversed with many who had seen Christ, but was also, by apostles in Asia, appointed bishop of the Church in Smyrna, whom I also saw in my early youth, for he tarried [on earth] a very long time, and, when a very old man, gloriously and most nobly suffering martyrdom, departed this life, having always taught the things which he had learned from the apostles, and which the Church has handed down, and which alone are true. To these things all the Asiatic Churches testify, as do also those men who have succeeded Polycarp down to the present time,—a man who was of much greater weight, and a more steadfast witness of truth, than Valentinus, and Marcion, and the rest of the heretics. He it was who, coming to Rome in the time of Anicetus caused many to turn away from the aforesaid heretics to the Church of God, proclaiming that he had received this one and sole truth from the apostles,—that, namely, which is handed down by the Church. There are also those who heard from him that John, the disciple of the Lord, going to bathe at Ephesus, and perceiving Cerinthus within, rushed out of the bath-house without bathing, exclaiming, "Let us fly, lest even the bath-house fall down, because Cerinthus, the enemy of the truth, is within." And Polycarp himself replied to Marcion, who met him on one occasion, and said, "Dost thou know me?" "I do know thee, the first-born of Satan." Such was the horror which the apostles and their disciples had against holding even verbal communication with any corrupters of the truth; as Paul also says, "A man that is an heretic, after the first and second admonition, reject; knowing that he that is such is subverted, and sinneth, being condemned of himself." There is also a very powerful Epistle of Polycarp written to the Philippians, from which those who choose to do so, and are anxious about their salvation, can learn the character of his faith, and the preaching of the truth. Then, again, the Church in Ephesus, founded by Paul, and having John remaining among them permanently until the times of Trajan, is a true witness of the tradition of the apostles.—Taken from *Ante-Nicene Fathers: History of the Christian Church,* Vol. I, page 416 by Irenaeus.

2. Make a list of all the warnings that John gives in this epistle.
3. Underline each time John uses the word "love." What does he teach about love in this epistle?
4. Read through 2 and 3 John in one sitting. Compare the style and content of each (e.g., 2 John 1 and 3 John 1; 2 John 4 and 3 John 4; 2 John 12 and 3 John 13-14). Compare 1 John with 2 and 3 John (e.g., 1 John 4:3 and 2 John 7).

UNIT 1—The Word of Life/1 John 1:1-4

TEXT

The Word of Life

1 That which was from the beginning, which we have heard, which we have seen with our eyes, which we have looked at and our hands have touched—this we proclaim concerning the Word of life. [2]The life appeared; we have seen it and testify to it, and we proclaim to you the eternal life, which was with the Father and has appeared to us. [3]We proclaim to you what we have seen and heard, so that you also may have fellowship with us. And our fellowship is with the Father and with his Son, Jesus Christ. [4]We write this to make our[a] joy complete.

[a]4 Some manuscripts *your*

STUDY

READ

Two readings of the passage are suggested—each with a response to be checked or filled in on the worksheet.

First Reading/First Impressions: To get familiar with the Scripture passage as though you are reading the passage for the first time, and to record your "first impressions" on the worksheet.

Practice: Read through the entire letter (in a modern translation) and check two boxes that best describe the *tone* or *mood* of this letter.

☐ Scholarly—like a professor

☐ Fatherly—like a parent

☐ Diplomatic—like a politician

☐ Friendly—like an alumni newsletter

☐ Pious—like a devotional writer

☐ Formal—like a IRS form letter

☐ Tender—like a love letter

☐ Sober—like a bank officer

☐ Stern—like a Marine drill sergeant

☐ Long-winded—like a preacher

Second Reading/Theme or Headline: To get the overall idea, thought or "gist" of the passage, as though you are seeing the action from the press box, high above the stadium.

Practice: Read the first four verses (1 John 1:1-4) and check the boxes that come the closest to describing the "big idea" in this passage. (Choose two)

☐ Are you ready for this?

☐ God has a better idea

☐ Check it out

☐ Oh what a feeling

☐ Fellowship is what it is all about

☐ Reach out and touch

☐ Who said you can't have it all?

☐ Just one look. That's all it took

☐ Let the good times roll

☐ I'm gonna make you an offer you can't refuse

SEARCH

On what basis does the apostle John say in verse 1: "*. . . that which we have seen and heard, which we have seen with our eyes, which we have looked at and our hands have touched . . .*"? Look up the following verses and jot down what each contributed to his first hand experience.

1. John leaves John the Baptist to follow Jesus: John 1:35-39 (John usually referred to himself as the "other" disciple or did not mention his name)

2. John is present at the transfiguration. Mark 9:2-13

3. John is with Jesus at Gethsemane. Mark 14:32-42

4. John is present at the crucifixion of Jesus. John 19:26-27

5. John discovers the empty tomb. John 20:1-9

6. What is the significance of the ways John personally experienced "the Word"? (vv. 1-2)

7. Given why John wrote this letter (vv. 3-4), what do you expect to gain from studying it?

APPLY

As you begin this course, what are some goals you would like to work on? Check one or two from the list below and add anything specific in the box.

☐ To get to know God in a more personal way
☐ To understand what I believe as a Christian and where I stand on issues
☐ To develop my skills in Bible study and personal devotions
☐ To belong to a small group that will support me in my growth
☐ To think through my values and priorities in light of God's will
☐ To wrestle with the next step in my spiritual journey with others who care

What are you willing to commit to in the way of disciplines during the time you are in this course?

☐ To complete the Bible study home assignment before the group meets
☐ To attend the group meetings except in case of emergency
☐ To share in leading the group—taking my turn in rotation
☐ To keep confidential anything that is shared in the group
☐ To reach out to others who are not in a group and invite them in
☐ To attend the teaching session with the pastor/teacher

GROUP AGENDA

Every group meeting has three parts: (1) gathering (15 minutes) for coffee and announcements, (2) sharing (30-45 minutes) for Bible study, and (3) caring (15 minutes) for prayer requests and prayer. When you get to the SHARING/BIBLE STUDY, divide into groups of four (4 at the dining table, 4 at the kitchen table, etc.) and use the flow questions below.

TO BEGIN/10 Minutes (Choose 1 or 2)

☐ What was special to you about your room in the first house you lived in? ☐ What childhood memory is as clear today as the day it happened? ☐ What person you met as a child made a lasting impression on your life? ☐ What did you jot down under READ?

TO GO DEEPER/15 Minutes (Choose 2 or 3)

☐ If you did not go over the Introduction (pp. 9-11) in the Orientation Session, take a few minutes to share its highlights with the group. ☐ Go around your group and answer the questions under SEARCH on your worksheet—one person answering question 1, the next person answering question 2, etc. ☐ Why does John make a point of his firsthand experience with Jesus? Why is it important that Jesus was "seen" and "touched"? ☐ Case History: Mary calls you to say she is attending a Meditation Workshop sponsored by a New Age group because she realizes her need for a spiritual center for life. From your experience, what could you honestly share with her about what you have found regarding spiritual reality?

TO CLOSE/5 to 20 Minutes (Choose 1 or 2)

☐ Discuss what you jotted down under APPLY on your worksheet. How can you help each other reach the goals you set? ☐ Can you remember the first time God became more than just a name to you?

NOTES ON 1 JOHN 1:1-4

Summary . . . John begins his letter with a prologue that is reminiscent of the prologue to his gospel (John 1:1-18). Both prologues focus on the preexistent Word of God who has been revealed to humanity. In each there are the themes of "life" and "witness." In each, there is the visual manifestation of God to the "we" who then proclaim what has been experienced. But there are also differences between the two prologues. In the gospel prologue, the emphasis is on the divine nature of the Word. Over half the verses make this point. But in the prologue to 1 John, the divine nature of the Word is simply noted. Instead, the emphasis is on the *physical manifestation* of the Word of God. This difference in emphasis is due to the difference in audience. In his gospel John wrote to Jews who did not believe that God could or would reveal himself in the person of Jesus. But here in the epistle, the secessionists presuppose that Jesus is the Son of God. Their problem is that they neglect his human side. This is why John emphasizes the fact that the preexistent Word of life has been experienced by auditory, visual, and manual means. The Word really became flesh—real flesh.

Although the prologue in 1 John is only four verses long, it is a very complex piece of writing. In Greek this is a single sentence which is, according to one scholar, a "grammatical tangle" (Dodd). For one thing, John reverses the normal sentence order. Usually in a sentence the subject comes first, followed by the verb and then its object. But here John puts the *object* first. In verse 1, he begins with four relative clauses (which are the objects of the verb), each introduced by the word "which." Then, to complicate matters even more, verse 2 is really a parenthesis which describes the nature of the "Word of life." It is only in verse 3 that John finally gets around to his main verb ("we proclaim"). Because he has taken so long to identify the main verb, he finds it necessary

to repeat in verse 3 the essence of what he has already said in verse 1. In an attempt to clarify all this, the translators of the NIV have inserted a verb in verse 1.

This structure, however, is not haphazard. It has a distinct purpose. In this way John is able to focus attention on the object which is proclaimed (Jesus Christ) rather than on the act of proclamation itself.

v. 1 . . . Although this document lacks the usual identification of sender and recipient, as well as the normal greeting and prayer, it is clear that this is not an anonymous tract written to a general audience. Scattered throughout the letter are abundant personal comments and specific references (e.g., 2:19). This letter was written to particular people living at a particular place who were dealing with specific problems. (For an example of how New Testament letters generally begin, see 1 Peter 1:1-2 and Philippians 1:1-2).

which . . . John begins with four clauses, each introduced by "which." The first clause describes who the "Word of life" is. The next three describe how he was experienced.

from the beginning . . . The initial clause makes the astonishing assertion that this "Word of life" was preexistent. He always existed. (Compare John 1:1). Since only divine beings preexisted, in this way John affirms the diety of Jesus.

heard/seen/touched . . . However, John's emphasis is on the human nature of Jesus. The next three clauses describe how his physical presence was experienced. This eternal "Word of life"

took on a form so specific and so concrete that he could be known by means of each of the higher senses. Notice the progression of experience. In the Old Testament, men and women had on many occasions *heard* God; occasionally they had *seen* some aspect of God (see Exodus 3:1-6; 33:18-23); but no one had ever *touched* God. This was the final proof that the Word of life had indeed been "made flesh and dwelt among us" (John 1:14, KJV).

In Greek courts, the testimony of two senses was required in order to verify that something occurred (Brown). John offers evidence from a third sense as well. He emphasizes as strongly as he can the physical existence of Jesus because of the secessionists lack of interest in the earthly Jesus.

touched . . . This word means literally "to feel after" or "to grope" as a blind person might do. It also means "to examine closely" (Brooke). Jesus was no phantom. He was a real person whose skin could be touched.

Word of life . . . This phrase refers both to the message preached by the early Christians and to the content of that message. The message preached by the apostles and by Jesus himself concerned eternal life, i.e., spiritual life—that which people do not naturally possess but which must be given them by God. This is one sense of the phrase "Word of life." But Jesus not only preached this message. He was the message. This is a second sense of the phrase. The "Word of life" was preached to people, which was that Jesus Christ was the Word of God, the very embodiment of eternal life itself (see John 1:4; 11:25-26; 14:6).

v. 2 ... This is a parenthesis in which John declares in unequivocal terms that *Jesus* is the Word he is talking about.

we ... The author is amongst those who knew Jesus personally.

testify ... This is a legal term describing what an eyewitness does while in court. Such a person makes a public declaration of what he or she has experienced firsthand.

the eternal life ... This is a curious way by which to refer to Jesus. Yet in this way John focuses on what is so significant about Jesus: he is life itself. God's very life has appeared in the historical person of Jesus (see John 1:2).

v. 3 **we proclaim** ... This is the main verb of the opening sentence. It clarifies the intention of the prologue. John's aim is to identify the nature of the apostolic proclamation, which is that Jesus is the incarnate God.

fellowship ... This word means literally in Greek, "having in common." It has the dual sense of first, *participation together* in shared activity or outlook, and second, *union together* because of this shared experience. The aim of John's testimony is to bring others into participation and union with him and his colleagues, and thus into participation and union with the Father and the Son. The secessionists proposed a different sort of union (or communion). Their emphasis was on direct union with God, whereas John

emphasizes communion not only with God but with others. John identifies a triangular pattern of relationship (God, self, others) in contrast to their vertical pattern (God and self).

with the Father and with his Son ... Apparently the false teachers were saying that it was possible to have fellowship with God apart from Christ. John's point is that fellowship with God is possible only through Jesus (2:23) because in him eternal life (i.e., God's life) is manifested.

v. 4 ... John identifies his second reason for writing. He wants his own joy to be completed.

joy ... This is the profound gladness or satisfaction that comes when one participates in the life of God. This is an important term for John. He uses it 9 times in his gospel (along with an additional 9 times that he uses the verb "rejoice"). See, for example, John 15:11; 16:20, 22, 24; and 17:13, each of which promises joy. In John 20:20 he indicates that the fulfillment of this promise is found in the experience of the resurrected Lord. Here in 1 John he goes one step further and indicates the joy which began with the experience of the resurrected Lord is brought to completion via the experience of this full-orbed fellowship between Father, Son and the children of God. The children of God include the apostles and those who have believed the good news which they proclaimed about Jesus.

complete ... full, lacking nothing.

COMMENTS

Seeing is Believing ... But Touching is Better

When John says that they not only heard and saw Jesus, but actually touched him, we understand what he is saying. He is asserting in the strongest possible experiential language that Jesus had a real body. Jesus was no phantom or will-of-the-wisp. He was not "materialized spirit." He was not an illusion. He was real like we are real. His was a flesh and blood body with smooth skin, real muscles, eyes that stared back at you, and with hair that had to be combed. He was flesh and blood.

It is necessary for John to make this point because of the secessionists who are troubling his church. They wanted their Jesus to be fully divine. They wanted God. They were not so sure about man. Of course they knew that Jesus had been a man—sort of. But this is not what they liked about Jesus. What they liked was his diety and all he could teach them about the supernatural.

The problem with their view (it was later labeled docetism and condemned as a heresy) was that in downplaying Jesus' humanity, they minimized his atoning work. They minimized his dying for sins. They minimized sin. And so this view could not be allowed to stand. If Jesus did not die for our sins as a real man (who was sinless) then we are still in sin—cut off from God and lost. This was no minor theological error. This is the kind of misunderstanding that undercut the very heart of Christianity.

It is important to know this. 2000 years later there are those folk among us who say that the America church has once again become docetic. We don't deny Jesus was human, but the fact is that what we like most about him is his divinity. This is still a problem. In losing sight of his humanity we cut ourselves off from all that he can teach us about our own struggle to become fully human.

UNIT 2—Walking in the Light/1 John 1:5-2:2

TEXT

Walking in the Light

[5]This is the message we have heard from him and declare to you: God is light; in him there is no darkness at all. [6]If we claim to have fellowship with him yet walk in the darkness, we lie and do not live by the truth. [7]But if we walk in the light, as he is in the light, we have fellowship with one another, and the blood of Jesus, his Son, purifies us from all[a] sin.

[8]If we claim to be without sin, we deceive ourselves and the truth is not in us. [9]If we confess our sins, he is faithful and just and will forgive us our sins and purify us from all unrighteousness. [10]If we claim we have not sinned, we make him out to be a liar and his word has no place in our lives.

2 My dear children, I write this to you so that you will not sin. But if anybody does sin, we have one who speaks to the Father in our defense—Jesus Christ, the Righteous One. [2]He is the atoning sacrifice for our sins, and not only for ours but also for[b] the sins of the whole world.

[a]7Or *every*   [b]2Or *He is the one who turns aside God's wrath, taking away our sins, and not only ours but also*

STUDY

READ

First Reading/First Impressions

This passage strikes me as . . . □ a manifesto of the Christian life. □ a back and forth argument. □ a pastor's letter to encourage the church. □ a simple passage that is really very complex.

Second Reading/Big Idea

What verse seems to you to be the controlling verse of this section? Why?

SEARCH

1. What does John mean by his statement "God is light"? (v. 5)

2. Verses 6-10 are a series of "if" statements. What is the condition and result in each instance?

	Condition	Result
(v. 6)		
(v. 7)		
(v. 8)		
(v. 9)		
(v. 10)		

3. From these statements, what does it mean practically to "walk in the light"? (v. 7)

4. What modern day example might you use to explain 2:1-2 to someone unfamiliar with the Old Testament ritual of atonement? (See Leviticus 16:6-22, 34.)

APPLY

Paraphrase. From now on in the APPLY part of the worksheet, you will be asked to try a different form of application in each unit. In this unit, we want you to try rewriting a verse of Scripture in your own words. This will force you to think through the meaning as you struggle to write your own modern translation.

Go back and read verse 9—phrase by phrase. Close your eyes and try to restate the thought of this verse in *your own everyday speech,* like you were explaining this idea to your next door neighbor.

Then, in the space below, write your own original expanded translation. For instance, *"If we honestly and sincerely own up to the fact that we have goofed . . . done wrong . . . made a mistake . . . broken God's law . . . etc."*

Be creative. Be original. And use a little "literary license" if you wish, but get the main idea of verse 9 across.

What help do the following verses give you as you deal with sin in your life?

(1:9)

(2:1-2)

GROUP AGENDA

Remember, every group meeting has three parts: (1) gathering (15 minutes) for coffee and announcements, (2) sharing (30-45 minutes) for Bible study, and (3) caring (15 minutes) for prayer requests and prayer. When you get to the SHARING/BIBLE STUDY, divide into groups of four (4 at the dining table, 4 at the kitchen table, etc.) and use the flow questions below.

TO BEGIN/10 Minutes (Choose 1 or 2)

☐ Are you afraid of the dark? ☐ What do you do when a movie gets scarey? ☐ What movie deserves an Oscar for blurring the line between right and wrong? ☐ Who came to your defense when you got in trouble as a kid? Who interceded for you? ☐ What did you jot down under READ on your worksheet?

TO GO DEEPER/15 Minutes (Choose 2 or 3)

☐ Go around and share what you jotted down under SEARCH on your worksheet—one person taking question 1, the next person taking question 2, etc. ☐ From what is said in this passage, what do you think the false teachers were trying to teach about God? about sin? about fellowship? ☐ This letter provides three tests for the Christian life: (a) the moral test, (b) the social test, and (c) the doctrinal test. Which test is discussed here and what is the conclusion? ☐ Case History: Judy has a problem with guilt. Spiritually she cleaned house last year, but she keeps hearing voices from her past life, reminding her of her sin. How would you help Judy deal with her guilt?

TO CLOSE/5-20 Minutes (Choose 1 or 2)

☐ What did you write down for the paraphrase in APPLY? ☐ How about in the second question? ☐ Looking over this past week, do you feel like your life spiritually was like a stormy night? Or a day with no clouds? Or a partially cloudy day? Why?

17

NOTES ON 1 JOHN 1:5-2:2

Summary . . . In the prologue John declares his hope that all may be in fellowship with God and with each other. Here in these verses he examines the barrier that prevents such fellowship (sin) and how to deal with it. By means of a series of "if/then" clauses (with the "then" implied) he identifies three erroneous views of sin which he then evaluates on the basis of the fact that God is light. His pattern of writing is to begin a sentence with "if" and then state the false view and its detrimental consequences (verses 6, 8, 10). He then starts a new sentence, again with the word "if," within which he states the correct view (verses 7, 9, 2:1b).

v. 5 **from him** . . . John is quite clear about the source of his message. What he preaches comes directly from Jesus, taught to him as one of the Twelve. In contrast, the secessionist's wisdom is derived from inner, subjective visions (as implied in 4:1-3).

God is light . . . This is John's second great assertion about God. His first assertion was that *God had come in the flesh* (vv. 1-3). Here he states that *God is light*. Within contemporary Greek culture, "light" was a common symbol for God. It conveyed the idea of wisdom, integrity, excellence, etc. Within the context of the Bible, "light" was connected to two basic ideas. First, on the intellectual level, it was a symbol of *truth*. John is saying that God is truth. God illuminates the understanding of people. He reveals the right answer and the correct way (see Psalm 27:1 and Proverbs 6:23). Second, on the moral level, light is a symbol of *purity*. John is saying that God is righteous and holy (see Isaiah 5:20, Ephesians 5:8-14, and Romans 13:11-14).

He is good, not evil. The coming of Jesus was, therefore, the coming of light (see Matthew 4:16, John 1:4-9; 3:19-21). Jesus is "the light," as John says in his gospel. He is the incarnation of the divine light (John 8:12, 9:5). This insight into the nature of God stands in sharp contrast to the many "dark gods" known in the first century world who were given over more to evil than to good.

v. 6 **If we claim** . . . This is the first of three false claims that John will refute. He will measure the validity of each of these claims against the apostolic proclamation that God is light and in him is no darkness.

to have fellowship . . . yet walk in the darkness . . . False claim number one is that it is possible to be in union with God and yet habitually sin. That this cannot be so is clear from what John has just stated about God. If God is *light* then, by definition, those who walk in *darkness* cannot be part of him. This was a common gnostic error. They felt that since the body was insignificant, then it did not matter what a person did. The true essence of the person—the "spirit"—remained untouched and thus uncontaminated by sin.

we lie . . . John moves from the false proposition (that they have fellowship with God even while living in darkness) to the inevitable conclusion (they are not telling the truth). To say that one can practice sin and still be in fellowship with God is simply not true.

v. 7 **But if** . . . Having identified the false proposition of the secessionists in verse 6,

John now states the true proposition in verse 7.

walk in the light . . . The image here is of a person confidently striding forth, illuminated by the light of God's truth, in contrast to the person who stumbles around in darkness. To "walk in the light" is to be open and transparent. It is "to be, so to speak, all of a piece, to have nothing to conceal, and to make no attempt to conceal anything" (Stephen Neill).

purifies . . . If the first result of "walking in the light" is fellowship with one another, the second result is cleansing from sin. That which causes the blemish of sin to disappear is the sacrificial death of Jesus. (This is what the symbol of "blood" refers to.) It is through the death of Jesus that sin is forgiven and forgotten. The verb tense here indicates that this purification occurs not just once but is a continuous process.

v. 8 **If we claim to be without sin** . . . This is false claim number two: that they are sinless. It is one thing to deny that sin breaks fellowship with God (as in verses 6 & 7). At least then the existence of sin is admitted even if its impact is denied. But it is another thing to deny the fact of sin altogether. This might have been the response of the secessionists to John's assertion (in verse 6) that because they walked in the darkness of sin they could have no fellowship with God. "But," they would protest, "this cannot be so. We do not walk in the darkness of sin. In fact, we have no sin at all." They might claim that they are without sin for one of two reasons: either because they felt that sin had to do with the body and the body had nothing to do with "fellowship with God."

One fellowshipped with God via the "spirit" and by their own definition, no sin could or did taint their spirit. Or they could have felt that as a result of the special esoteric knowledge they had about God, they had been cleansed from all sin and granted perfected natures.

we deceive ourselves . . . This assertion goes beyond a mere lie (v. 6). This is self-deception. They really believed they were without sin.

the truth is not in us . . . Not only do they not live by the truth (v. 6), but by such a claim they demonstrate that they do not even know the truth (as found, for example, in Romans 3:23—"all have sinned.") Again, this demonstrates that they are not part of God, who is light, and who therefore stands for truth.

v. 9 **If we confess our sins** . . . As in verse 7, after naming the problem John then states the antidote. Rather than denying their sinful natures they need to admit their sin to God and so gain forgiveness.

faithful . . . God will keep his promise to forgive (Micah 7:18-20).

just . . . The granting of forgiveness is not just an act of unanticipated mercy but a response of justice, since as a result of the death of Christ the conditions for forgiveness have been fulfilled.

purify . . . Sin makes a person unclean; forgiveness washes away that sin (see verse 7).

v. 10 **If we claim we have not sinned** . . . This is false claim number three: not only do they say that at the present moment they are without sin (v. 8), they actually claim never to have sinned! The secessionists might admit that sin does break fellowship with God (v. 6) and that all people have an inborn sinful nature (v. 8), but they would still deny that they, in fact, have ever actually sinned.

we make him out to be a liar . . . God's verdict is that all people are sinners. Furthermore, he says that it is through the death of Christ that he forgives sin. So by claiming sinlessness they are, in essence, saying that God is lying about human nature and about his claim to forgive people.

his word has no place in their lives . . . They claim to know God and yet they do not walk in his way nor accept his viewpoint about human nature. Therefore, contrary to what they might claim, they are, in fact, alienated from God (see John 8:44).

2:1-2 . . . Here is the antidote to the third and final error of John's opponents. John alters the structure of his sentence slightly by placing the "if" in the middle of his statement and not at the beginning, but it is clear that he is responding to the assertion that they have never sinned.

v. 1 **dear children** . . . This is literally "small children," an affectionate term for his congregation which John uses frequently (2:12, 28; 3:7, 18; 4:4; 5:21). At this point in his letter John shifts his focus from the secessionists and their heresy to his own flock and their needs.

so that you will not sin . . . Having just stated that Christians are not free from sin (v. 10), John runs the risk of being misinterpreted. People might say: "Since sin is always with us and since forgiveness is freely offered, then why not sin?" (see Romans 6:1). Thus John quickly points out that sin is not compatible with Christian commitment.

if anybody does sin . . . While urging sinlessness as a goal to strive for, John knows that in this present life this cannot be achieved. So the issue then is how to deal with sin. The answer is found in the triple role of Jesus as the advocate, the righteous one, and the atoning sacrifice.

one who speaks . . . in our defense . . . This is how the NIV translates the single Greek word, *parakletos*. It means, literally, "one called alongside" and usually carries the idea of one who is called upon to help. Here the idea is that since people have no basis on which to ask for forgiveness, Jesus does so on their behalf.

Righteous One . . . John frequently refers to Jesus by means of this term (e.g., 2:29; 3:7). Jesus is righteous both in the sense of being an example to follow and, especially, in the sense of not being contaminated by personal sin.

v. 2 **the atoning sacrifice** . . . Jesus, the advocate, has as the basis for his plea (that their sin should be forgiven) the fact of his death in their place for their sin. Such a sacrifice is effective because he himself was without sin (the Righteous One) and so could take the place of another.

TEXT

³We know that we have come to know him if we obey his commands. ⁴The man who says, "I know him," but does not do what he commands is a liar, and the truth is not in him. ⁵But if anyone obeys his word, God's love is truly made complete in him. This is how we know we are in him: ⁶Whoever claims to live in him must walk as Jesus did.

⁷Dear friends, I am not writing you a new command but an old one, which you have had since the beginning. This old command is the message you have heard. ⁸Yet I am writing you a new command; its truth is seen in him and you, because the darkness is passing and the true light is already shining.

⁹Anyone who claims to be in the light but hates his brother is still in the darkness. ¹⁰Whoever loves his brother lives in the light, and there is nothing in him^a to make him stumble. ¹¹But whoever hates his brother is in the darkness and walks around in the darkness; he does not know where he is going, because the darkness has blinded him.

^a10 Or *it*

STUDY

READ

First Reading/First Impressions
My sense here is that John . . . □ is stating the obvious. □ is deeply profound. □ has succeeded in distilling the essence of Christianity. □ is confusing me.

Second Reading/Big Idea
What's the main point or topic?

SEARCH

1. What connections can you find between obeying, knowing, and loving God in verses 3-6? (See also John 14:15, 21, 23-24.)

2. Since the false teachers were bringing "new insights" to these people, what does John mean by stressing that his command is not "new"? (v. 7)

3. From Mark 12:28-31 (also Leviticus 19:18; Deuteronomy 6:5) and John 15:12, 17, what is this "old command" to which John refers? (See also 3:11; 2 John 5.)

4. From what you can recall from the gospels, what are a couple ways Jesus made this "old" command new? (v. 8)

5. What does John's linking of "love/light" and "hate/darkness" together (vv. 9-11) imply about:

having a relationship with God?

spiritual maturity?

what holiness is all about?

APPLY

Measuring yourself by the tests of verses 3, 6 and 10, what grade would you give yourself for Christian living this week? _____ What is one specific way these verses challenge you to improve your relationships?

Self Inventory. Here is another form of application. Take inventory of the relationships in your life and put a dot on the lines below to indicate how you are feeling right now about each of these relationships—somewhere between the two extremes. For instance, you might put the dot on YOUR PERSONAL LIFE right in the middle because you are halfway between "Blues In the Night" and "Feeling Groovy."

IN MY PERSONAL LIFE, I'M FEELING LIKE...
Blues In the Night _____Feeling Groovy

IN MY FAMILY LIFE, I'M FEELING LIKE...
Stormy Weather _____The Sound of Music

IN MY WORK, SCHOOL OR CAREER, I'M FEELING LIKE...
Take This Job and Shove It _____Everything's Coming Up Roses

IN MY CLOSE RELATIONSHIPS, I'M FEELING LIKE...
Nowhere Man _____You Light Up My Life

IN MY SPIRITUAL LIFE, I'M FEELING LIKE...
Mickey Mouse Disco_____Hallelujah Chorus (Messiah)

GROUP AGENDA

Divide into groups of 4 before starting on these questions. Stick to the time limits and ask the groups to "move on" to the next phase.

TO BEGIN/10 Minutes (Choose 1 or 2)

□ What was the standard line you got from your parents when you went out in the evening during high school? (Behave yourself. Be careful. Drive slowly. Don't be late.) □ As a child, were you afraid of the dark? What "monsters" were in it that scared you? □ What did you write for READ?

TO GO DEEPER/15 Minutes (Choose 2 or 3)

□ Go around your group and explain your answers under SEARCH on the worksheet— one person taking question 1, the next person question 2, etc. □ This passage outlines both the "moral" and "social test" of being a Christian (see notes on vv. 3-6 in the Summary—p. 22). Without using "religious" language, how could you explain these "tests" to someone just exploring the Christian faith? □ What do you think is going on in the church to cause John to write this? □ Case History: Bob has a problem with a grudge against his old business partner. They were in a Bible study group and decided to go into business together. Bob had the money. His partner had the idea. The business went sour and Bob lost his investment. Bob grumbles aloud that his partner mismanaged the business and tampered with the books to hide his mistakes. What do you say to Bob?

TO CLOSE/5 to 20 Minutes (Choose 1 or 2)

□ What did you write for APPLY? □ How do you react to a Christian who "talks" a little more than he "lives"? □ As you get older, do you find it easier or harder to forgive your close friends and family? □ Where do you need to try a little love this week?

NOTES ON 1 JOHN 2:3-11

Summary . . . John now shifts his focus. He had been addressing the secessionists by way of refuting their false claims. Now he addresses his own flock, exhorting them to follow God's commands. He does, however, point out several additional false claims (see verses 4, 6, and 9) within the context of his discussion of the commandment to love. Within this unit John identifies two "tests" by which people can be certain they actually know God: the test of obedience and the test of love. Those who truly know God live in his way and love as Jesus loved.

vv. 3-6 . . . Thus far John has presented two truths about God which lie at the heart of the apostolic proclamation and by which the accuracy of ideas and actions are to be judged. These are, first, the . . .
. . . historical manifestation of the Eternal and secondly . . . the fact that God is light . . . All Christian profession may be judged in relation to these truths. No thought or action can be condoned which is inconsistent either with God's nature as pure, self-giving, or with His historical palpable self-disclosure in Christ . . . This general introduction . . . is now particularized in three tests—moral (the test of obedience), social (the test of love) and doctrinal (the test of belief in Christ). (Stott)

The first application of the moral test is here in verses 3-6.

v. 3 **We know** . . . The New English Bible translates this opening phrase: "Here is the test by which we can make sure we know him. . . ."

v. 3 **have come to know him** . . . Previously John has spoken about *having fellowship*

with God (see 1:3, 6, 7). Now he speaks about the parallel concept, that of *knowing God* (see 2:4, 13, 14; 3:6, 16; 4:16). The verb tense here indicates that he is thinking about a past experience ("we *have come* to know him").

if we obey his commands . . . The first test as to whether a person knows God, therefore, is moral in nature: does that person keep God's commands? To know God is to live in his way. The secessionists claim to know God but, as John will show, they live in a way that belies that claim.

commands . . . The nature of these commands is not spelled out but the context (vv. 7-11) indicates that John probably had in mind the "great commandment" to love God and love others (Mark 12:29-31). Whatever their specific definition may be, these commands are not some external semi-arbitrary set of rules which must be obeyed simply because they exist. These commands describe the way Jesus lived (see 2:6). They are the very pattern of the Life that John is talking about. They are what love looks like in a person's life. Unless the commands are seen in this way they will degenerate into dead ethical propositions.

v. 4 **The man who says** . . . John identifies another false claim. Those who assert that they really "know God" and yet do not keep his commandments are, in fact, lying. Such a man demonstrates by what he does that what he says is false.

does not do . . . The emphasis here is on sins of omission (not doing) in contrast to

1:6 where the emphasis is on sins of commission (walking in darkness).

v. 5 **God's love** . . . This is the reward for obedience. God's love reaches its fulfillment in that person's life.

made complete . . . The verb which John uses here means ongoing fulfillment rather than static termination.

v. 6 . . . Here John introduces the idea of the "imitation of Christ." Christians are habitually to live the way Jesus lived. He is their model. As he walked, so should they walk.

live in him . . . This is the third phrase which John uses to describe union with God. (In 1:3 he used the phrase "having fellowship with God" and in 2:3 he spoke about "knowing God.") To "exist in" God or to "abide in" him "suggests an intensely personal knowledge of God; it presupposes an intimate and committed relationship with him, through Jesus, which is both permanent and continuous" (Smalley).

vv. 7-11 . . . If the first test of whether one is actually a Christian is moral in nature (Do you obey God?), then the second test (given here), is relational in orientation (Do you love others?).

v. 7 **dear friends** . . . This is literally "beloved," and is derived from the word "love" *(agape)* which is John's focus in this section.

I am not writing you a new command . . . This is not a new commandment because Jesus himself had stated it some years earlier and the Johannine Christians themselves had been taught it right from the beginning of their Christian walk. It is also not new in that when Jesus gave this command he was, in fact, quoting the Old Testament. He combined Leviticus 19:18 and Deuteronomy 6:5 to form the "great commandment."

command . . . John switches from the plural in verse 3 to the singular here since all commands are, in fact, summed up in the one great commandment (John 13:34).

v. 8 **Yet I am writing you a new command** . . . The commandment is *new* in the sense that Jesus tied together two previously separate commands (that of loving God and loving others) and broadened their application (Christians are to love everyone, not just those in their own group as shown in the parable of the Good Samaritan in Luke 10:30-37).

its truth is seen in him and you . . . It is also new in that it was only in recent years that the commandment was actually lived out by Jesus and his followers. In them one *saw* (instead of just read about) this new kind of love (see John 10:14-18; 15:9-17).

darkness/light . . . Howard Marshall explains the concept here this way:
> The newness of the commandment lies in the fact that it is being fulfilled in a way that had not happened previously. To put it differently, the darkness of the old age, in which men did not love in this sort of way, is disappearing, and the light of the new age, in which Christian love is shown, is already shining. The picture is that of a world in the darkness of night, but the first rays of the dawning sun have already begun to shine; more and more areas are becoming light instead of dark, and the light is getting brighter. There are still dark places, completely sunk in shadow, but there are places where there is bright light, and it is here that the disciples are to be found, walking in the light and themselves shedding light." (Marshall)

true light . . . This is genuine light, in contrast to the false "light" claimed by the secessionists. This is "true light" because what it appears to be is what it actually is. Nothing is hidden. Nothing is dark.

vv. 9-10 **light/love** . . . John here links sets of contrasting images: light and darkness with love and hate. Those who are in the light, love. Those who are in the darkness, hate. In other words, enlightenment goes hand in hand with active care for others.

v. 9 **claims** . . . Another false claim—that a person can actually be in God's light and yet hate others.

brother . . . John's primary focus here is on love and hate within the Christian community. However, the relationships between people in the church ought to be a model for all relationships.

v. 10 **love** . . . The Greek word John uses here is *agape*. In Greek there are several words that can be translated by the English word "love." There is one word for sexual attraction or sexual desire *(eros);* another for family love, affection, and friendship *(philia).* In contrast, agape refers to self-giving sacrificial action done on behalf of another who is in need, regardless of what it might cost ("Greater love has no one than this, that one lay down his life for his friends"—John 15:13) or what is felt about that other person ("Love your enemies"—Luke 6:27).

stumble . . . This word refers to a "trap" or a "snare" that causes one to fall into sin or error.

v. 11 **hates** . . . If a person does not love, that is, does not care for the needs of another in direct, active ways, then such a person hates. It is either love or hate in John's view. He does not offer neutrality as a comfortable third option in relationships. In the same way that when John talks about love he is thinking about deeds not feelings; so too, "hate" has little to do with feelings of hostility toward others. "Hate" is the lack of loving deeds done on their behalf.

walks around in the darkness . . . When people live in the light, they can see where they are going. But those who reject God's viewpoint simply stumble blindly through life, bumping into all sorts of things, hurting others and hurting themselves.

blinded . . . Living apart from God's way (i.e., "in darkness") will yield over time moral and spiritual blindness so that it becomes difficult for one to see what is and is not true or good. Hatred distorts perception.

UNIT 4—Stages of Faith/1 John 2:12-17

TEXT

¹²I write to you, dear children,
   because your sins have been forgiven on
      account of his name.
¹³I write to you, fathers,
   because you have known him who is from
      the beginning.
I write to you, young men,
   because you have overcome the evil one.
I write to you, dear children,
   because you have known the Father.
¹⁴I write to you, fathers,
   because you have known him who is from
      the beginning.
I write to you, young men,
   because you are strong,
   and the word of God lives in you,
   and you have overcome the evil one.

Do Not Love the World
   ¹⁵Do not love the world or anything in the
world. If anyone loves the world, the love of the
Father is not in him. ¹⁶For everything in the
world—the cravings of sinful man, the lust of
his eyes and the boasting of what he has and
does—comes not from the Father but from the
world. ¹⁷The world and its desires pass away,
but the man who does the will of God lives
forever.

STUDY

READ

First Reading/First Impressions
What's going on here? □ Maybe John is quoting a song. □ Maybe some copyist wrote this material down twice. □ Maybe John is repeating himself for emphasis.

Second Reading/Big Idea
What verse seems most important here for you? Why?

SEARCH

1. What are the characteristics of each of the three stages of maturity described in verses 12-14?

2. In your own words, how would you describe the "children" stage today? (vv. 12-13)

3. In your own words, how would you describe the "young men" stage today? (vv. 13-14)

4. In your own words, how would you describe the "fathers" stage today? (vv. 13-14)

5. What are two or three other words you would substitute for the word "love" in verse 15?

6. How have the three forms of "love for the world" (v. 16) manifested themselves in your experience?

7. What are the two options a Christian has and what is the end result of each option? (v. 17)

Option 1

Option 2

APPLY

In your spiritual life, in what ways do you feel like a . . .

a "child"—just beginning to catch on to this?

a "young man"—at the peak of strength in this?

a "father"—a seasoned veteran in this?

What form of the world is the biggest threat to your spiritual growth now? □ Inner desires fighting to be unchecked. □ An absorption with material things. □ Pride over your past accomplishments. What is one way you can nurture the love of God in your life instead?

GROUP AGENDA

Divide into groups of 4 before starting on these questions. Watch the time limits and ask the groups to "move on."

TO BEGIN/10 Minutes (Choose 1 or 2)

□ What nickname did your parents have for you as a child that you would do a slow burn over if anyone called you now? □ Who is the person that saves all the pictures of your family to show off at family reunions? □ What TV commercial deserves an Oscar for portraying the exact opposite of what Christ calls us to be? □ What did you jot down under READ?

TO GO DEEPER/15 Minutes (Choose 2 or 3)

□ Go around your group and explain your answers under SEARCH on the worksheet— one person taking question 1, the next person question 2, etc. □ Make a study of the verbs in verses 12-14. What does the tense of the verb describing children, young men and fathers reveal about their spiritual development? □ How would you describe in today's terms the lifestyle of these Christians? □ What, if any, is the difference between the lifestyle of these Christians? □ Case History: Jeff, a recent college graduate, is trying to figure out his priorities regarding finances. There are so many things he needs and wants, but he is also aware of his responsibility to support the church and care for the poor. From your experience, how would you help him sort through the love "of the world" versus the love of God?

TO CLOSE/5-20 Minutes (Choose 1 or 2)

□ What did you write in APPLY? □ What encouragement for Christian living do you get from these verses? □ What sign would you choose to describe what's going on in your life right now? ("Under New Management" "Danger! Under Construction" or "Please Be Patient. God Isn't Through With Me Yet")

NOTES ON 1 JOHN 2:12-17

Summary . . . In contrast to those who walk in darkness—and about whom John has just been writing (2:9-11)—in this unit he turns to those who are committed to the light. He has two things to say to the Christian community. First, he assures them of their standing before God (vv. 12-14); and second, he warns them about loving the world (vv. 15-17). It is worth noting that up to this point in his epistle John has always led off his argument by first stating *false* claims, but here his focus is on *true* claims.

vv. 12-14 . . . In six parallel and almost poetic statements John addresses three groups of Christians by using the terminology of a family. It is not completely clear to whom John is referring with the titles "children," "fathers," and "young men." In fact, he may not have actual groups in mind and is simply thinking about different stages of the spiritual life (the innocence of childhood, the strength of youth, and the mature knowledge of age, as Augustine put it). Some scholars feel that John is addressing the whole community by means of the term "dear children," much as the wisdom teachers of Old Testament addressed their followers. And then he speaks to two groups of believers within the community of "dear children:" those who have been Christians for a long time (the Fathers) and those who are newer members of the faith (the young men).

v. 12 **children** . . . John affirms two foundational truths: they are forgiven (v. 12) and they do know God (v. 13b). It is important that the Christians in John's church be assured that this is true for them. The secessionists are claiming that *they* have experienced forgiveness and that *they* know God but John has rejected

their claims (1:6-10; 2:4). Lest his own flock fear their claims to such reality are also being rejected, John assures them that they are in a different place from the secessionists. Here he reaffirms that the walk of faith begins with these two experiences.

have been forgiven . . . The verb tense here indicates that John is thinking of the forgiveness that comes at the time of conversion; whereas in 1:9 his concern was with ongoing forgiveness for subsequent sins based on the confession of sins.

name . . . In the Near East a name is very significant. It is not just a convenient word for distinguishing one person from another. It is a description of the essential character of that person. Thus the name Jesus recalls not just who he is but his atoning work through which forgiveness has been made possible (1:7, 2:1-2).

v. 13 **fathers** . . . John Stott has this to say about this word:

> [These are the] spiritually adult in the congregation. Their first flash of ecstasy in receiving forgiveness and fellowship with the Father was an experience of long ago. Even the battles of the young man, to which he will next refer, are past. The fathers have progressed into a deep communion with God. (Stott).

you have known him . . . The message to the "fathers" here and in verse 14 is identical. John reassures them that they do, indeed, know Christ. Once again John uses the perfect tense for the verb. In this way he emphasizes the present consequences of a past event. This same

tense is used for each of the main verbs in the six messages.

him who is from the beginning . . . The reference is probably to Jesus since it echoes the phrase by which John opens his letter: "that which was from the beginning" which is a direct reference to Jesus.

young men . . . John asserts that the Christian life involves spiritual warfare. To be a Christian does not merely entail the enjoyment of sins forgiven and a warm relationship with God. It is also a vigorous battle against evil.

overcome . . . "Overcoming" is an important theme in all of John's writing. (See John 16:33; Revelation 2:7f.; and 1 John 4:4; 5:4f.) In the same way that Christ overcame Satan via his death and resurrection, so too Christians are to overcome the evil one. Twice the "young men" are commended for showing themselves to be spiritually strong enough to have overcome Satan (vv. 13 & 14)."

the evil one . . . Satan, the ruler of darkness (see verses 8-11) and the source of evil.

children . . . In Greek, a different word is used here for "children" than is used in verse 12. In verse 12 the word is *tekna* and emphasizes the kinship that exists between children and parents. Here, the word is *paidia*. It emphasizes the age of children, i.e., they are young and in need of training. However, these distinctions are minor and are more ones of nuance than substance.

you know the Father . . . Not only do Christians experience the forgiveness of sins (see verse 12a), they also enter into a personal relationship with God.

v. 14 word of God . . . This is the source of the overcoming power displayed by the "young men." They know God's will and have lived in conformity to it.

lives in you . . . The word of God is meant not only to be understood but it is also intended to be incorporated into a person's very being.

vv. 15-17 . . . Having just assured his hearers about their secure relationship with God, John now finds it necessary to warn them about an attitude that could bring them down, lest they now feel themselves immune from the power of evil. The attitude they are to avoid is "love of the world." John bases his command on two factors: the incompatibility of love for God with love for the world (vv. 15-16) and the transience of worldly desires in comparison to the everlasting life of those who do God's will (v. 17).

vv. 15-16 . . . John's plea in these verses is not for Christians to hate the material world or those people who live in it. As John noted in his gospel, God himself declared his love for the world: "For God so loved the world that he gave his one and only Son . . ." (John 3:16). Rather, what John is saying is that Christians must not give in to those temptations offered by a tainted world system. John is attacking an attitude ("love of the world"). He is not attacking "things" *per se,* much less people. He condemns this attitude because it causes people to misuse what

God has created and what, therefore, is good. Furthermore, to be preoccupied with the pursuit of pleasure makes people insensitive to God's love. In fact, it makes it impossible for them to love at all since love is laying down one's life (1 John 3:16) and not possessing what is craved. Love for God and love of the world are mutually exclusive since both become all engrossing, consuming passions (see Matthew 6:24; James 4:4).

v. 15 love . . . As in verse 5 and verse 10, the love about which John speaks is not so much an emotional response as it is the act of caring expressed by what a person does. As such, this "love" is appropriately directed toward God (v. 5) and toward others (v. 10), but it is not to be expressed toward the pleasures of the world.

world . . . The word John uses here is *kosmos* and in this context it means that which is alienated from God and is, in fact, contrary to who God is. It refers to pagan culture which has abandoned God. "Our author means human society insofar as it is organized on wrong principles and characterized by base desires, false values, and egoism" (Dodd).

v. 16 everything . . . As John pointed out in his gospel, it is God who created the world: "Through him all things were made; without him nothing was made that has been made" (John 1:3). Therefore, John cannot mean that *everything* in the world is automatically evil. And indeed, by means of the three examples in this verse it becomes evident that what he has in mind are those aspects of the world that stand in active opposition to God's ways. Still, as Marshall puts it: "The language

may seem exaggerated, but it is timely: *anything* in the world can become a source of sinful desire, even though it is good in itself."

cravings . . . That part of human nature which demands gratification—be it for sexual pleasure, for luxury, for possessions, for expensive food, for whatever.

lust of the eyes . . . Greed which is aroused by sight. A person sees something and wants it. (For examples of this, see Genesis 3:6; Joshua 7:21; and 2 Samuel 11:2-4.)

boasting . . . Pride in one's possessions; an attitude of arrogance because one has acquired so much. In its original Greek usage this word referred to a man who claimed to be important because he had achieved so much when, in fact, he really had done very little. These three attitudes are interconnected. "Selfish human desire is stimulated by what the eye sees and expresses itself in outward show" (Marshall). Taken together they add up to a materialistic view of the world.

v. 17 pass away . . . To give oneself over to the love of the world is foolish because the world with its values and goods is already passing away (v. 8). Those who love the world will pass away with it while those who love God will live forever.

lives forever . . . In contrast to those who live for the moment are those who give themselves to eternal, unchanging realities. Eternal life is one of God's gifts to the Christian.

UNIT 5—Warning Against Antichrists/1 John 2:18-27

TEXT

Warning Against Antichrists

[18]Dear children, this is the last hour; and as you have heard that the antichrist is coming, even now many antichrists have come. This is how we know it is the last hour. [19]They went out from us, but they did not really belong to us. For if they had belonged to us, they would have remained with us; but their going showed that none of them belonged to us.

[20]But you have an anointing from the Holy One, and all of you know the truth.[a] [21]I do not write to you because you do not know the truth, but because you do know it and because no lie comes from the truth. [22]Who is the liar? It is the man who denies that Jesus is the Christ. Such a man is the antichrist—he denies the Father and the Son. [23]No one who denies the Son has the Father; whoever acknowledges the Son has the Father also.

[24]See that what you have heard from the beginning remains in you. If it does, you also will remain in the Son and in the Father. [25]And this is what he promised us—even eternal life.

[26]I am writing these things to you about those who are trying to lead you astray. [27]As for you, the anointing you received from him remains in you, and you do not need anyone to teach you. But as his anointing teaches you about all things and as that anointing is real, not counterfeit—just as it has taught you, remain in him.

[a]20 Some manuscripts *and you know all things*

STUDY

READ

First Reading/First Impressions
John here is like a . . . □ doomsday prophet. □ parent giving lecture #101. □ wise old owl speaking from experience. □ leader angry at others who disagree with him.

Second Reading/Big Idea
In your own words, how would you express what you think is the key verse here?

SEARCH

1. What is John referring to when he says, "This is the last hour..."? (v. 18)

2. From verses 19 and 22, how would you recognize an antichrist if you met one? (See also 4:3; 2 John 7)

3. By contrast, what do these verses imply are the marks of a true Christian?

4. How would you explain what John means by "the anointing"? (vv. 20, 27; see also John 14:17; 15:26; 16:13)

5. What does John mean by "acknowledging" the Son? (See 1:3, 7; 2:1-6; 4:2, 15)

6. In verse 27, does John mean they have no need of teachers at all, or that there are no "new" truths they need to learn besides what the apostles taught? Why?

APPLY

Common thread. This approach is similar to the approach used in the last unit. Instead of taking one passage and milking everything you can from that passage on a subject, you look for the "common thread" that runs through the whole passage.

In this case, we want you to look for the "three tests" for a Christian that have been presented in this chapter, and jot down what you find for each test in your own words.

THE MORAL TEST (1 John 2:3-6)

THE SOCIAL TEST (1 John 2:7-11)

THE DOCTRINAL TEST (1 John 2:18-28)

GROUP AGENDA

Divide into groups of 4 before starting on these questions. Watch the time recommendations and ask the groups to "move on."

TO BEGIN/10 Minutes (Choose 1 or 2)

☐ What do you crave that is either "illegal, immoral, or fattening"? ☐ What did you put down for READ? ☐ In what field do you consider yourself something of an expert? Who was one person that really helped you master the "basics" of that field? ☐ Who was your favorite teacher in high school? Why?

TO GO DEEPER/15 Minutes (Choose 2 or 3)

☐ Go around your group and explain your answers under SEARCH on the worksheet— one person answering question 1, the next person question 2, etc. ☐ Reading between the lines, what do you think is going on? ☐ According to the definition of antichrist in this passage, what modern day movements would fall into this category? ☐ What is going to keep a person from being led astray? ☐ Case History: Your friend Ron tells you that he is really excited about Jesus, but wants nothing to do with the church. "The church is full of hypocrites who have nothing to teach me. Besides, I've got the Spirit now so who needs some minister telling me what I have to believe? My job is to spread his message, not to sit and listen to boring sermons." What could you share about the importance of remaining with the church from your own experience?

TO CLOSE/5 to 20 Minutes (Choose 1 or 2)

☐ Share what you jotted down under APPLY. ☐ Who was a spiritual parent to you, who cared enough to warn you when you were about to go astray? How is their help to you a model of how you might help someone else? ☐ What insights have you gained so far from 1 John about recognizing true from counterfeit Christianity?

NOTES ON 1 JOHN 2:18-27

Summary . . . Having assured the members of his church that they are, indeed, walking in the Christian way, John returns to the question of how to distinguish between those who are true Christians and those who are counterfeit Christians. Thus far in his epistle he has defined two tests which enable one to make such a distinction: the true Christian is obedient to God's commands (the moral test, verses 3-6) and the true Christian loves other people (the social test, verses 7-11). Now he adds a third test: the true Christian remains firmly committed to the truth of God. This is the doctrinal test (Stott).

vv. 8 **the last hour** . . . The early Christians understood clearly that the first coming of Christ (the incarnation) inaugurated "the last days." They also knew that his second coming (the *parousia*) would bring to a close the "last days" and usher in a new age in which God's rule would be visible and universal. In the first century the expectation was that this second coming of Jesus would take place in the immediate future. It could, in fact, happen at literally any moment. In this passage one catches this sense of urgency. "The time is short," John is saying, "this is the last hour. He is coming back. So be ready." It is almost as if a clock is ticking away the final moments before the Second Coming.

But, of course, the Second Coming did not occur during John's lifetime nor in the following 18 centuries. How can this be? J. H. Newman has a fascinating answer. He says that the course of events was altered by Christ's coming in the flesh. Up until then . . .

the course of things ran straight towards the end, nearing it by every step; but now, under the Gospel, that

course has altered its direction, as regards His second coming, and runs, not towards the end, but along it, and on the brink of it; and is at all times near that great event. . . . Christ is ever at our doors (quoted by Bruce).

antichrist . . . Although John is the only New Testament writer to use this term (see 2:22; 4:3; 2 John 7), the same concept is present in other parts of Scripture (e.g., Mark 13:22 and 2 Thessalonians 2:1-12), namely that one day an opponent to Christ will arise who is the incarnation of evil and Satan—just as Christ was the incarnation of good and God.

antichrists . . . John points out that the coming of the antichrist was not just some future threat. Even at that moment the "spirit of the antichrist" (see 4:3) was loose in the world and active in those who deny Christ and his teachings (see verse 22).

v. 19 **they went out from us** . . . John now identifies those who are imbued with the spirit of the antichrist. They are none other than the secessionists who left the church and even now seek to win over their former friends and colleagues to their point of view (see verse 26).

none of them belonged to us . . . John distinguishes between the visible church (which consists of those who participate in church activities) and the invisible church (those who also belong to Christ). The two groups are not necessarily the same. "External membership is no proof of inward union" (A. E. Brooke). One of the distinguishing marks of the true Christian is perseverance. It is not that salvation is the reward of perseverance

but rather that endurance is a characteristic of those who are true Christians. By leaving the church, the secessionists revealed their true status.

v. 20 **an anointing** . . . In the Old Testament, when a king or a priest was consecrated to God's service, oil was poured on them as part of the ceremony. Here the noun refers to the *means of anointing,* namely the Holy Spirit. Just as Jesus was anointed with the Holy Spirit (Luke 4:18; Acts 10:38) so too is the believer. The Holy Spirit is thus the one that guides the Christian into all truth (John 14:17; 15:26; 16:13).

all of you . . . In contrast to the secessionists who claimed to have special, esoteric insight into spiritual truth not available to others (this was the source of their new doctrine), John assures his readers that *all* Christians know the truth, not just an elite few.

you know the truth . . . The departure of the secessionists from the church was not the only evidence that "they did not really belong to us." The Christians already knew that they espoused false doctrines by virtue of their Holy Spirit derived insight into what was true.

v. 21 . . . John does not offer any "new truth" in this epistle. He simply confirms for his readers what they already know to be true. His aim is to reassure them in the face of the claims being made by the secessionists that they already have the truth.

no lie comes from the truth . . . John's reasoning is this: true Christians have the Holy Spirit and therefore know the truth (v. 20). Those who know the truth do not lie (which is what he says here). Therefore, the implication is that those who are lying by teaching false doctrine do not know the truth because they do not have the Holy Spirit and thus they are not true Christians.

v. 22 . . . John now reveals the master lie in the secessionists' false teaching: they deny that Jesus is the Messiah and the Son of God. This is an obvious lie that all true Christians will immediately recognize.

The antichrists probably taught (as some later Gnostics certainly taught) that Jesus was born and died a man, and that "the Christ," by which they meant a divine emanation, was within Him only during His public ministry, descending upon Him at His baptism and leaving Him before the cross. They thus denied that Jesus was or is the Christ or the Son. They made Him a mere man invested for a brief period with divine powers or even adopted into the Godhead, but they denied that the man Jesus and the Eternal Son were and are the same Person, possessing two perfect natures, human and divine. In a word they denied the incarnation (Stott).

v. 23 . . . The Father and the Son are inseparable. To deny the Son is to deny the Father (despite what might be claimed). Likewise, to confess the Son is to confess the Father (see John 10:30). This is the awful effect of the secessionists' heresy: to deny Jesus makes fellowship with God impossible.

denies/acknowledges . . . These are the only two options when it comes to Jesus. The idea here is of public confession and public denial (see Matthew 10:32-33; John 12:42; Romans 10:9, 10).

v. 24 **See that** . . . John now issues a command. In the face of the lies of the antichrists they are to remain faithful to the word of God.

what you have heard from the beginning . . . As an antidote to heresy, John urges his readers to let the original message which they heard right from the start of their Christian lives control their perspective. By urging them to remain faithful to the original apostolic word preached to them, he is ruling out private revelation that would deny or contradict this message—revelation such as the secessionists' new doctrines.

remain . . . John's point is that when they remain in the truth they will remain in fellowship with God. To "remain" . . . expresses a continuing relationship. It is not enough merely to have heard and assented to the message in time past. The message must continue to be present and active in the lives of those who have heard it. They must continually call it to mind and let it affect their lives (Marshall).

v. 25 **eternal life** . . . What has been promised the Christian is the sharing of the very life of God—both now in the present (beginning at conversion) and on into the future after death (John 3:36; 6:40, 47; 17:3).

v. 26 **lead you astray** . . . John now reveals more about the secessionists. They were not simply content to leave the church and form their own fellowship based on their private doctrines. Instead, they actively sought to make converts from amongst the Christian community.

v. 27 . . . The ultimate safeguard against heresy is the Word of God which has been conveyed to their hearts by the Spirit with whom they have been anointed (Marshall).

remains in you . . . In verse 24 the stress was on the activity of Christians to ensure that they remained faithful to the Word of God which they heard from the beginning. Here the complementary truth is expressed: by God's grace Christians do remain in this teaching. Human response and divine activity are both part of the Christian life.

teach . . . John is not saying that after anointing by the Holy Spirit Christians need no more instruction. John is, in fact, instructing them via this letter! What they do not need is instruction by the false teachers.

all things . . . This is not "everything that can be known," but rather "all that you need to know."

vv. 24-27 . . . "Here, then, are the two main safeguards against error—the apostolic Word and the anointing Spirit. Both are received at conversion. 'You heard' the Word (v. 24) he says, and 'you received' (v. 27) the Spirit, although, indeed, he implies, the Word has come to you from us (1:2, 3, 5), while you have received the Spirit direct of, that is from, *him,* 'the Holy One' (vv. 27, 20). The Word is an objective safeguard, while the anointing of the Spirit is a subjective experience; but both the apostolic teaching and the Heavenly Teacher are necessary for continuance in the truth. And both are to be personally and inwardly grasped" (Stott).

UNIT 6—Children of God/1 John 2:28-3:10

TEXT

Children of God

²⁸And now, dear children, continue in him, so that when he appears we may be confident and unashamed before him at his coming. ²⁹If you know that he is righteous, you know that everyone who does what is right has been born of him.

3How great is the love the Father has lavished on us, that we should be called children of God! And that is what we are! The reason the world does not know us is that it did not know him. ²Dear friends, now we are children of God, and what we will be has not yet been made known. But we know that when he appears,ᵃ we shall be like him, for we shall see him as he is. ³Everyone who has this hope in him purifies himself, just as he is pure.

⁴Everyone who sins breaks the law; in fact, sin is lawlessness. ⁵But you know that he appeared so that he might take away our sins. And in him is no sin. ⁶No one who lives in him keeps on sinning. No one who continues to sin has either seen him or known him.

⁷Dear children, do not let anyone lead you astray. He who does what is right is righteous, just as he is righteous. ⁸He who does what is sinful is of the devil, because the devil has been sinning from the beginning. The reason the Son of God appeared was to destroy the devil's work. ⁹No one who is born of God will continue to sin, because God's seed remains in him; he cannot go on sinning, because he has been born of God. ¹⁰This is how we know who the children of God are and who the children of the devil are: Anyone who does not do what is right is not a child of God; neither is anyone who does not love his brother.

ᵃ2Or *when it is made known*

STUDY

READ

First Reading/First Impressions
What old proverb best catches the idea of this passage? □ Like father, like son. □ Birds of a feather flock together. □ One rotten apple spoils the barrel. □ You can tell a man's character by the company he keeps.

Second Reading/Big Idea
What are some earlier passages in 1 John that remind you of this section?

SEARCH

1. What do the following verses indicate about the motives and reasons for living a holy life?

(2:28)

(2:29)

(3:1-3)

(3:6)

(3:9)

2. What verses show the inner qualities that characterize a person "born of God"? (Example: joy—3:1)

3. From verse 6, does John mean a Christian cannot sin? Will not habitually sin? Will not deliberately sin? Why?

4. Do you think verses 6 and 10 were meant to promote self-inspection or to give them a standard to judge true from false teaching? Why?

5. From 3:1, 6, 9, and 10, what are the sources of tension between Christians and "the world"?

APPLY

Summary. This form of application is just the opposite of paraphrase (which you have already done). This time, instead of *expanding* the Scripture into your own modern translation, you *condense* the passage into a few words. This forces you to look for the essential teaching and boil it down into a few words. See if you can condense this passage into 50 words or less.

Of the motives given in SEARCH question 1, which one most spurs you on? Why?

GROUP AGENDA

Divide into groups of 4 before starting on these questions. Stick to the time limits.

TO BEGIN/10 Minutes (Choose 1 or 2)

☐ Whose coming would motivate you to get busy and clean house—your boss? your in-laws? your small group? ☐ When you were a child, were you more motivated to obey your parents by threats or promises? ☐ What did you put down for READ? ☐ What is one of your parent's characteristics that you definitely have inherited?

TO GO DEEPER/15 Minutes (Choose 2 or 3)

☐ Go around your group and explain your answers under SEARCH on the worksheet—one person taking question 1, the next person question 2, etc. ☐ From what John says, what do you think the false teachers were teaching? ☐ What is the difference between verse 6 in this passage and 1 John 1:8? ☐ Case History: Bob became a Christian about a month ago. He was quite the ladies' man before. Sexually active. Fast living. Heavy drinking. Suddenly, his whole life has started to change. His old friends are mystified. Mad. "Bob has got religion," they say, "but it won't last." Bob is discouraged by this ridicule, and wonders if his friends are probably right. How would you encourage him?

TO CLOSE/5 to 20 Minutes (Choose 1 or 2)

☐ Share what you jotted down under APPLY. ☐ As you get older, do you find the old sinful desires easier or harder to resist? ☐ When you blow it, what have you found most helpful in making it right with God and getting on with life? ☐ How does it make you feel that one day you will be "like Jesus"? (v. 2)

NOTES ON 1 JOHN 2:28-3:10

Summary . . . In the previous unit John articulated the third and final test that distinguishes a cult from a Christian church. In the next three units (found in 2:28 to 4:6) he will go back over these three tests a second time. In this unit (2:28-3:10) he reexamines the moral test by discussing obedience once again. In the next unit (3:11-24) he reexamines the social test by discussing once again what is involved in loving other people. In the final unit (4:1-6) he reexamines the doctrinal test by pointing out again the correct view of Jesus.

2:28-3:3 . . . In the previous unit (2:18-27) John urged his readers to resist the proselytizing of the dissenters and to remain in Christ. In these verses he continues to urge his readers to remain in Christ, but now the reason he gives has to do with the Second Coming of Christ. If they remain in Christ, when they meet the Lord at the Second Coming they will not be ashamed. Instead, they will be confident before the Lord (2:28). Furthermore, they know that they will see Christ as he is and be made like him (3:2). The Second Coming is thus a source of great hope for the Christian and an encouragement to holy living (3:3).

v. 28 continue . . . The word translated here as "continue" is the same Greek word that was translated "remain" in 2:19, 24, and 27. It can be translated in a variety of ways: "to abide," "to remain steadfast," "to dwell," "to rest," "to persist," "to persevere," or "to be intimately united to." However the best rendering is "to remain" or "to abide in."

appears . . . This is the same word that is used in 1:2 to describe the incarnation of Jesus. Here it describes his Second Coming. The word carries with it the idea of that which was once invisible now being made visible.

confident and unashamed . . . On the Day of Judgment (which will occur at the Second Coming) those who have rejected Christ will feel a sense of unworthiness and shame in the presence of his holiness (Isaiah 6:5) and because of their open disgrace at having rejected Christ. In contrast, Christians will be able boldly to approach the royal presence because they have lived their lives in union with Christ.

v. 29 everyone who does what is right . . . One consequence of spiritual rebirth is right living. It is, in fact, a sign of rebirth as the child begins to display the characteristics of his or her father.

born of him . . . Thus far John has described Christians as those who "have fellowship with the Father and with his Son" (1:3); as those who "know God" (2:3, 4, 13, 14); as those who are "in Christ" (2:5, 6); as those who are "in the light" (2:9, 10); and as those who "abide" in the Father and the Son (2:24, 27, 28). Now he offers yet another description of what it means to be a Christian. Christians are those who experience "spiritual rebirth." He thus defines the relationship between the believer and God by means of the analogy of the relationship between a child and a father. (See also 1 Peter 1:3, 23; Titus 3:5).

3:1 . . . The precise nature of what Christians will become when they meet Christ is not fully clear ("what we will be has not yet been made known"). Yet they can get an idea of what they will be like by looking at Jesus ("we shall be like him"). In some way Christians will become like Jesus when the process of glorification—which began at conversion/rebirth—is completed at the Second Coming.

v. 3 . . . Christians purify themselves in anticipation of Christ's return.

this hope . . . Namely, that one day Christ will appear again at which time they will see him as he really is and be changed so as to become like him.

pure . . . This is a common word in the Bible denoting the outward purity required of those persons or objects involved in temple worship. In the usage here it speaks of the moral purity (freedom from sinning) that is required of Christians. Such purification is necessary for those who are in union with Christ. The secessionists, in contrast, were not much concerned about sin (1:5-2:2).

vv. 4-10 . . . Having stated that those who are Christians and who have the hope of the Second Coming as their motivation for purifying themselves, John next looks at the sin from which they must purify themselves. In these verses he addresses the negative: the children of God must *not* sin. In 3:11-24 he will address the positive: instead, the children of God are to love one another.

v. 4 . . . John now defines sin (it is lawlessness) and the sinner (everyone who breaks the law).

lawlessness . . . It is not completely clear what John means when he says that "sin is lawlessness." Some scholars feel that what he is saying is that "sin consists of breaking the law of God." Other scholars feel—because of how this word is used in 2 Thessalonians 2:3, 7—that what John is saying is that "sin is placing oneself on the side of the 'man of lawlessness' " (i.e., Satan)—and thus standing in rebellion against God. Sin in this second sense is "siding with God's ultimate enemy!" (Marshall).

v. 5   ... John gives yet another reason for not sinning. The very purpose for Jesus coming in the first place was to take away sin. So it is obvious that Jesus stands over against sin. Furthermore, there was no sin in Jesus' life. The implication is that those who are in union with Christ will reflect this same abhorrence of sin.

in him is no sin ... John asserts that Jesus was sinless. His testimony is all the more powerful even though this is not his main point. John is not trying to prove anything. He is simply stating what he knows to be true. And John was in a position to know whether Jesus was actually without sin because he lived with Jesus for some three years. Those who live with us know us best. Yet John says—after having seen Jesus in a variety of situations over a three year period—that Jesus is *without sin*.

v. 6   ... John appears to be saying here (and in verses 8-10) that a Christian *cannot* sin. Yet in other passages he points out that Christians can and do sin (e.g., 1:8, 10; 2:1; 5:16). Some scholars feel that what John has in mind here is willful and deliberate sin (as against involuntary error). Other scholars stress the tense of

the verb that John uses: a Christian does not *keep on* sinning. In other words, Christians do not habitually sin. Still other scholars feel that what John does here is to point out the ideal. This is what would happen if a Christian abided constantly in Christ. In any case, "John is arguing the incongruity rather than the impossibility of sin in the Christian" (Stott).

v. 7   **lead you astray** ... The secessionists deny that there is any incompatibility between being a Christian and continuing in sin. In other words, they not only seek to lead Christians away from the truth (2:26), they also seek to lead them into an immoral lifestyle.

righteous ... It is not enough simply to *claim* to be righteous. The true Christian *does* what is right.

vv. 8-10 ... In these verses John restates what he has said in verses 4-7. This statement parallels his previous statement except that here the focus is on the origin of sin (it is of the devil) rather than on the nature of sin (it is breaking the law).

v. 8   **of the devil** ... Just as Christians display their father's nature by moral living, so too others demonstrate by their immoral lifestyles that Satan is really their father.

sinful ... In verse 4 sinfulness was described as lawbreaking. Here sin is linked with Satan who from the beginning has sinned.

to destroy the devil's work ... Satan seeks to harm the body, mind and soul of human beings. Physically, he inflicts disease; intellectually he seduces into

error; and morally he entices into sin (Stott). Jesus sets himself over against all this. He seeks to undo and to thwart the harm Satan would bring. (See especially John 12:31 and also Matthew 4:1-11; 12:25-28; Luke 10:18; Revelation 12:7-12; 20:1-3.)

v. 9   **cannot go on sinning** ... In 1:8, 10, and 2:1 John attacks those who deny that they are sinners in need of forgiveness (i.e., those who are blind to the fact of their sin). Yet here he seems to say that Christians cannot sin. Some scholars feel that in chapter one John was responding to one aspect of the pre-gnostic heresy of the secessionists—i.e., their teaching that those who were spiritually enlightened were perfect. But here he is dealing with a second aspect of that heresy—i.e., the teaching that sin did not matter. To those holding the first view he declared the universality of sin (all are sinners). Here, in the face of the second error, he declares the incompatibility of sin with the Christian life.

God's seed ... John probably is referring either to the Word of God (see Luke 8:11; James 1:18; 1 Peter 1:23) or to the Holy Spirit (see John 3:6) or to both, by which the Christian is kept from sin. In any case, "seed" is a metaphor for the indwelling power of God which brings forth new life.

v. 10   ... John here spells out in clear, unequivocal terms the moral test, although he casts it in *negative* terms: a person "who does not do right is not a child of God." He also articulates the social test—in anticipation of the next unit—again in negative terms: a person is not a child of God "who does not love his brother."

UNIT 7—Love One Another/1 John 3:11-24

TEXT

Love One Another

¹¹This is the message you heard from the beginning: We should love one another. ¹²Do not be like Cain, who belonged to the evil one and murdered his brother. And why did he murder him? Because his own actions were evil and his brother's were righteous. ¹³Do not be surprised, my brothers, if the world hates you. ¹⁴We know that we have passed from death to life, because we love our brothers. Anyone who does not love remains in death. ¹⁵Anyone who hates his brother is a murderer, and you know that no murderer has eternal life in him.

¹⁶This is how we know what love is: Jesus Christ laid down his life for us. And we ought to lay down our lives for our brothers. ¹⁷If anyone has material possessions and sees his brother in need but has no pity on him, how can the love of God be in him? ¹⁸Dear children, let us not love with words or tongue but with actions and in truth. ¹⁹This then is how we know that we belong to the truth, and how we set our hearts at rest in his presence ²⁰whenever our hearts condemn us. For God is greater than our hearts, and he knows everything.

²¹Dear friends, if our hearts do not condemn us, we have confidence before God ²²and receive from him anything we ask, because we obey his commands and do what pleases him. ²³And this is his command: to believe in the name of his Son, Jesus Christ, and to love one another as he commanded us. ²⁴Those who obey his commands live in him, and he in them. And this is how we know that he lives in us: We know it by the Spirit he gave us.

STUDY

READ

First Reading/First Impressions

From this passage, it seems that love . . . □ will conquer all. □ is all you need. □ makes the world go round. □ is like a flower and you its only seed. □ is the gift that keeps on giving.

Second Reading/Big Idea

If you had to reduce this passage to a slogan to fit on a T-shirt, what would you write?

SEARCH

1. From verse 11 and 2:7 (also 2 John 5), what must be going on that John again reminds the readers of what they have heard "from the beginning"?

2. Read the story of Cain and Abel in Genesis 4:1-8. How does the motive that lay behind Cain's actions apply to the way "the world" may treat Christians? (vv. 12-13)

3. If a person claims to be a Christian and still behaves like Cain toward a Christian brother, what news does John give this person? (vv. 14-15)

4. In contrast to Cain, what stands out to you about what real love involves? (vv. 16-18)

5. In the practical case John uses, what is the general principle to be applied? (v. 17)

6. How is loving others related to our . . .

assurance?
(v. 14)

(vv. 19-20)

(v. 24)

prayers?
(vv. 21-22)

7. Compare verse 23 with Galatians 5:6b. From these passages, how would you sum up what it means to be a Christian?

APPLY

What is one way you want to apply love "Jesus style" this week in your family, or at work, or in your community?

Written prayer. This is one of the simplest and most profound forms of application. Go back and read the passage again and try to rephrase this passage into a prayer—a very personal prayer. Start out with the words, *"Dear God, I . . ."* and go from there.

GROUP AGENDA

Divide into groups of 4 before starting on these questions. Note the recommended time limits and ask the groups to "move on."

TO BEGIN/10 Minutes (Choose 1 or 2)

☐ Who was your first "true love"? ☐ Who gave you your first kiss outside of the family? ☐ Have each member sing a line or two from their favorite love song and see who can correctly identify the most titles and artists. ☐ What did you jot down on your worksheet under READ?

TO GO DEEPER/15 Minutes (Choose 2 or 3)

☐ Go around and share what you jotted down on your worksheet under SEARCH—one person answering question 1, the next person question 2, etc. ☐ What do you think Christians in the first century were encountering from the non-Christian world? ☐ What kind of support were they giving each other? ☐ Case History: Jim has been out of work for two years. His unemployment insurance is gone and the bank has foreclosed on his house. His wife brings in a little money working part time but it isn't enough. They are proud people and won't ask for help but you know about their situation. What should you do?

TO CLOSE/5 to 20 Minutes (Choose 1 or 2)

☐ What did you write under APPLY? (Save sharing the prayers until you are ready to close.) ☐ Although we normally think of love in terms of personal relationships, how does the picture of love in verses 16-18 affect our involvement in social issues like racism or labor relations? Political issues like human rights and militarism? Foreign policy issues like Israeli/Palestinian concerns and aid to developing countries? Toward people or groups you really don't like? ☐ Do you know of anyone in your Christian community that needs your help at the moment?

NOTES ON 1 JOHN 3:11-24

Summary . . . The final verse of the previous unit (3:10) links together the idea of righeousness (the subject of that unit) and the idea of love (the subject of this unit). In that verse John says: "Anyone who does not *do what is right* is not a child of God; neither is anyone who *does not love his brother.*" By this statement John moves from the first test of orthodoxy (the moral test) to the second test (the social test) which he expounds in this unit.

This unit has two parts to it. In part one (verses 11-18) John states the second test: true Christians love one another. He demonstrates this first by means of a negative example (Cain) and then by means of a positive example (Jesus). Part two (verses 19-24) is a parenthesis in the flow of his thought in which he comments on assurance and on obedience, both in the context of prayer.

v. 11 This is the message . . . In 1:5 John used this same phrase to introduce the great truth that lies at the heart of the Christian message: God is light. Here he uses this phrase to introduce a second core insight: love is at the center of the Christian life. Those who seek to follow the God of light are called to a life of love.

you heard from the beginning . . . Once again (as in 2:7, 24) John reminds his readers that it was the teaching of the apostles that initiated and nurtured their faith. In contrast, the secessionists are urging the Christian to accept "new and advanced" doctrine.

love one another . . . This is a restatement of the second test (see also 2:9-11). Genuine Christians are those whose aim it is to live a life of love for others.

vv. 12-15 . . . John begins his exposition of love with a negative illustration: Cain's murder of his brother Abel.

Cain . . . Cain was the firstborn son of Adam and Eve. He was a farmer who gave an offering to God of "some of the fruits of the soil" (Genesis 4:3). His shepherd-brother Abel offered to God "fat portions from some of the firstborn of his flock" (Genesis 4:4). God was pleased with Abel's offering but not with Cain's. This made Cain very angry and in that anger, he killed his brother.

belonged to the evil one . . . Here John gives a specific example of what he meant in 3:8 when he said: "He who does what is sinful is of the devil." The killing of one's brother is the kind of evil that Satan inspires.

why did he murder him? . . . John answers this question in the next sentence: "Because his own actions were evil and his brother's were righteous." Cain knew that in contrast to his brother's gift, his offering to God did not arise out of the desire to do right. Therefore, because of his anger, Cain slew his brother.

v. 13 . . . Cain is an example of how evil hates righteousness. John warns the believers that wicked people will hate them too when they do good. The conclusion that John draws from this story is that Christians must expect hostility from the world (see 3:1 and John 15:18-25; 17:14; and 1 Peter 4:12-19).

v. 14 death . . . Here "death" refers to the kingdom of death—i.e., to the realm of Satan. In contrast, God's kingdom is characterized by life everlasting.

from death to life . . . The implication is that all people start out "dead." Satan is their father. They live in his realm. But by means of the rebirth process (which John mentioned in 2:29-3:2), it is possible to pass into the kingdom of life and become a child of God.

we know . . . because we love . . . Love is evidence that one possesses eternal life.

v. 15 Anyone who hates his brother is a murderer . . . Jesus makes this same link between hatred and murder (see Matthew 5:21-22). However, Jesus stopped short of saying what John does, namely, . . . that hatred is tantamount to murder.

vv. 16-17 . . . John next offers a positive example of love: Jesus' sacrificial love for the human race. Both the example of Cain and the example of Jesus involve death. But Cain's act sprang from *hatred* and *took* the life of another while Jesus's act sprang from *love* and he *gave* his own life for others.

v. 16 This is how we know what love is . . . John defines "love" not by means of an intellectual proposition but via a practical example. Love is what Jesus demonstrated when he gave his life for others. *Agape*-love, therefore, is self-sacrificial giving of oneself for the sake of others. *Agape*-love is not primarily an emotion. It is an action. This sort of love is called forth not by warm feeling for others, nor by obligations of kinship, but by the need of others.

v. 17 . . . While only a few Christians will be called upon to make the supreme sacrifice of their lives for the sake of others; *all* Christians can and must constantly share their possessions in order to relieve the material suffering that abounds in this world.

brother . . . In verse 16 John used the plural "brothers." But here he becomes quite specific and asks his readers to consider the needs of a particular individual ("brother" is singular). "Loving everyone in general may be an excuse for loving nobody in particular" (Lewis).

pity . . . Such self-giving love is not without emotion, even though it is not primarily a feeling. John calls for genuine concern in the face of the plight of others.

how can the love of God be in him? . . . "As life does not dwell in the murderer (v. 15), love does not dwell in the miser" (Stott).

v. 18 . . . But this "love" must be more than the mere verbal affirmation that "Yes, I am committed to the idea of love." Genuine love shows itself in concrete deeds and in truth.

vv. 19-24 . . . This section is a parenthesis in John's thought by which he both concludes the previous section and provides a bridge to the new unit. It is not easy, however, to follow John's thought-flow here as he links together the human and the divine aspects of assurance. The important thing to notice is that he is here talking about prayer.

vv. 19-20 . . . John seems to be saying that Christians can be at peace with themselves even when their consciences trouble them. Such troubled consciences may be the result of introspection that has pointed up how feeble their attempts are to love others and how prone to sin they seem to be. But, as John points out, the basis of their confidence is the fact that it is God who will judge them and not their own hearts. They can trust themselves to his all-knowing justice because they have sought and found his forgiveness (see 1 Corinthians 4:3-5).

v. 19 **truth** . . . By this word John links this new section to the previous section. People can only "belong to the truth" (v. 19)—i.e., be a part of God's kingdom, when they act "in truth" (v. 18)—i.e., when they love genuinely.

in his presence . . . The problem of a condemning heart would arise when a person was trying to pray.

v. 20 **whenever** . . . It is not an unusual experience for the conscience of a Christian to be troubled.

he knows everything . . . The human conscience is not infallible, but God is. The implication is that God—who knows a person's innermost secrets—will be more merciful than the heart of that person which sees in part and understands in part.

v. 21 **confidence** . . . Confidence is necessary in order to come before God. Without confidence a person does not feel free to enter into prayer.

v. 22 . . . Once again, John states a truth in a stark, unqualified way: if we ask, we will receive. Later, however, (in 5:13) he will add the proviso that people must ask "according to [God's] will."

obey . . . Obedience is not the *cause* of answered prayer; it is the condition that motivates Christians to pray. Obedience is the evidence that they are moving in accord with God's will; that they are in union with him; and that they will want to pray.

vv. 23-24 . . . In these verses John brings together the three issues which underlie the three tests by which believers can know they are truly children of God. He shows the interconnection between obedience (the moral test), love (the social test), and belief (the doctrinal test) and how these relate to the question of union with God.

v. 23 **to believe . . . and to love** . . . John here makes explicit what has previously been implicit: that at the core of Christianity there are two concerns—truth and love.

v. 24 **those who obey his commands live in him** . . . Obedience and union are connected. God's command is to believe and love. Obedience to this command brings union with Christ. Looked at from the other way around, union brings the desire and the ability to obey. In other words, the outward, objective side of the Christian life (which is active love for others in obedience to command of God) is connected to the inner, subjective experience of being in union with God.

how we know . . . The Holy Spirit is the source of the believers' assurance that God does, indeed, live in them (see 4:13).   39

TEXT

Test the Spirits

4 Dear friends, do not believe every spirit, but test the spirits to see whether they are from God, because many false prophets have gone out into the world. ²This is how you can recognize the Spirit of God: Every spirit that acknowledges that Jesus Christ has come in the flesh is from God, ³but every spirit that does not acknowledge Jesus is not from God. This is the spirit of the antichrist, which you have heard is coming and even now is already in the world.

⁴You, dear children, are from God and have overcome them, because the one who is in you is greater than the one who is in the world. ⁵They are from the world and therefore speak from the viewpoint of the world, and the world listens to them. ⁶We are from God, and whoever knows God listens to us; but whoever is not from God does not listen to us. This is how we recognize the Spiritª of truth and the spirit of falsehood.

ª6 Or *spirit*

STUDY

READ

First Reading/First Impressions
John reminds me here of a . . . ☐ teacher prepping students for the final. ☐ leader rebuking those who are not going along with his program. ☐ pastor encouraging the congregation that they are going to make it in spite of troubles.

Second Reading/Big Idea
Reading between the lines, what is going on that might prompt John to write this passage?

SEARCH

1. In your own words, what is the problem that John is addressing in this passage? (v. 1)

2. From 2:19, 22; 3:13, 23-24; 4:2 and 6, how do people motivated by God's Spirit differ from those motivated by other spirits in their attitudes towards:

Christ?

other Christians?

the world?

3. What hope does verse 4 provide for Christians as we face the pressures of dealing with falsehood?

APPLY

Verses 5-6 could be used by someone to accuse anyone who disagrees with "established opinion" of being false to the faith. What guidelines here and elsewhere in 1 John would help you distinguish between legitimate differences of opinion and heresy?

Topical study. This approach to application concentrates on one word or subject and gleans everything from the passage about this topic. In this case, we want you to make a study of cults. Study 2:18-27 and this passage writing out what characterizes (a) their origin (b) their teaching (c) their relationship to others and (d) the Christian's resources against them. First jot down the verse reference and the main idea it deals with. Then consider how what you found applies to one group today that proclaims "new" insights traditional Christians have "missed" (like the Jehovah Witnesses or an Eastern religion offshoot).

VERSE	MAIN IDEA

SUMMARY

GROUP AGENDA

Divide into groups of 4 before starting on the questions. Remember to follow the time recommendations.

TO BEGIN/10 Minutes (Choose 1 or 2)

☐ What big test made you nervous? (Your driver's test, a qualifying exam, an audition, a final in a course you had to pass) ☐ What did you put down for READ? ☐ Growing up, when was one time you remember thinking, "I wish I had just listened to what my parents said"?

TO GO DEEPER/15 Minutes (Choose 2 or 3)

☐ Go around your group and share the SEARCH portion of the Bible study—one person answering question 1, the next person taking question 2, etc. ☐ Who are the three pronouns in this passage referring to: "you" in verse 4, "them" in verse 5 and "we" in verse 6? ☐ If the false teachers denied that "Jesus Christ has come in the flesh," what were they teaching about Jesus? ☐ Case History: A college freshman returns from his first year at college with an obviously heightened awareness of spirituality. He has had contact with a number of Christian, Eastern, and "New Age" groups and is attracted by the sincerity and depth of commitment he sees in each. However, he is bothered by how the Christians reject the other's teachings whereas the others absorb Christian teaching into their own. What do you say when he asks you what you think about all this?

TO CLOSE/5 to 20 Minutes (Choose 1 or 2)

☐ What did you write for the first question in APPLY? ☐ What did you write about a contemporary cult? ☐ What guidelines can you use to discern between false teaching that undermines the faith and new insights that prophetically challenge how the faith applies to modern situations and problems?

NOTES ON 1 JOHN 4:1-6

Summary . . . In the final verse of the previous unit John describes how Christians can know that God lives in them. They know this because the Holy Spirit bears inner witness to this fact (3:24). But the problem is that the secessionists make this same claim! They say that God's spirit speaks to them too. In fact, such private revelations are the source of their new doctrine. So, how can one distinguish between spirits? What is the difference between God's Spirit and false spirits? Is there an objective basis on which to accept or reject subjective claims? The answer relates to doctrine. That spirit which acknowledges that Jesus (the Messiah) came in the flesh is a spirit from God. Likewise, the opposite is true. Those spirits that do not acknowledge Jesus in this way are not from God (see also 2:20-23).

Thus in this unit John expands on the doctrinal test—the third way by which to distinguish between true and false Christianity. There are two parts to this test. The first question is: to what spirit does one listen? Unless that spirit acknowledges Jesus as the Messiah come in the flesh, it is not of God (v. 2). The second question is: are you in submission to apostolic doctrine? Unless individuals acknowledge the truth of the gospel as taught from the beginning by apostles such as John they are not following "the Spirit of truth" (v. 6).

v. 1 do not believe every spirit . . . Having just claimed that Christians know God lives in them because the Holy Spirit bears witness to this fact, John hastens on to qualify what he means. Not everything a spirit says is automatically of God. In fact, it is dangerous to accept uncritically everything that is said "in the name of God." Not everyone claiming inner revelation is hearing God's voice!

test . . . The test that John suggests by which to distinguish between spirits is doctrinal in nature. It has to do with who Jesus is. False spirits will not acknowledge that Jesus of Nazareth (a fully human man) is the incarnate Christ (the divine Son of God). Notice that the focus of this test is upon the *spirit* who is the source of the prophecy—not upon *what* is said. In other words, true prophecy is not distinguished from false prophecy by the content of the prophecy itself. The question is: is the source of this prophecy divine or diabolical? (See also 1 Corinthians 12:1-3; 14:29; 1 Thessalonians 5:19-22).

spirits . . . The issue is not whether supernatural spirits exist and actually inspire prophecy. This was assumed to be the case by most everyone in the first century (see, for example, Mark 1:21-28, 32-34). The question Christians wrestled with was how to know *what kind* of spirit was speaking in any given situation. Are the secessionists telling the truth? Have they heard a fresh word from God? Did the Holy Spirit inspire this new doctrine? John provides them with a means whereby they can tell the difference between God's spirit and false spirits.

At first glance it might appear that John is dealing with the same issue that Paul discussed in 1 Corinthians 12 & 14. Paul talks there about "discerning spirits" and about how to bring order into a worship service in which there was a chaos of prophecy going on. (In the early church it was quite common for people—inspired by the Holy Spirit—to speak a word of prophecy on some other message during worship.) But Paul is "dealing with the problem of the order in which prophets

should speak and be heard, so that they should learn from one another" (Brown). These prophecies were all inspired by a "good Spirit." In John's case the problem is discerning good from evil spirits.

from God . . . John uses this phrase in five of the six verses in this unit. By it, in verses 1-3, he seeks to indicate that certain *spirits* have their origin in God (as opposed to others that emanate from "the antichrist") and in verses 4 and 6 he points out that certain *people* are of God (as opposed to others who are "from the world.")

prophets . . . Prophets are those men and women who claim to speak on God's behalf. They allow the Holy Spirit—or another spirit—to speak through them. John does not deny the reality or the value of prophecy. He simply warns against false prophets, much as Jesus did (See Matthew 7:15; Mark 13:22-23).

v. 2 . . . To deny that Jesus, the Messiah, was truly human is incompatible with divine inspiration. Prophets who will not affirm this confession of faith are not of God.

acknowledges . . . What John has in mind is not mere recognition of who Jesus is—since even the demons know him (Mark 1:24). Rather, what is called for is an open, positive, public declaration of faith in Jesus.

Jesus Christ has come in the flesh . . . This is the second of three places in this epistle in which John touches upon how the secessionists view the person of Jesus. In 2:22-23 John says that they deny that Jesus is the Christ (i.e., that he is the

Messiah). Here he asserts that they deny that Jesus, the Messiah, came in the flesh. In 5:6 (the third and final place at which he deals with the question of Jesus' nature) John gets to the heart of the matter. What the secessionists are really denying is that Jesus—as the Messiah—could have died.

Of course, it is difficult to know precisely what the secessionists believed about Jesus since we only have John's comments about them and nowhere does he lay out in a systematic fashion the nature of their beliefs. Some scholars feel that their views parallel those of Cerinthus, the gnostic heretic. If this is the case, the secessionists would have denied that the Son of God was truly in union with (i.e., one with) the human man whose name was Jesus. Rather, they would have said that the Divine Word of God temporarily indwelt human flesh, coming at the time of Jesus' baptism but leaving prior to his crucifixion. In any case, it seems likely that the secessionists would not have denied that Jesus was a human being (though they were uninterested in this fact because of their preoccupation with his deity). What they would deny (which becomes clear in 5:6) is that Jesus *as Messiah* actually died a human death.

v. 3   . . . In verse 2 John focused on the positive: those spirits who acknowledge Jesus are from God. Here he focuses on the negative: those who do not acknowledge Jesus are not from God.

antichrist . . . John returns to a theme he first dealt with in 2:18-27 (see the notes on 2:18). In that section John's concern was that believers not be led astray by those

who are filled with the spirit of the antichrist. Here his concern is with the claims by his opponents that their new teachings are inspired by God.

vv. 4-6 . . . John turns from his focus on prophets (true and false) to a consideration of those who follow each type of prophet. In verse 4 he directs his word to "you" (the Christians in Ephesus); in verse 5 he talks about "them" and "they" (the secessionists); while in verse 6 he talks about "we" (the apostles, of which John is a representative).

v. 4   **overcome** . . . The Christians to whom John writes have successfully resisted overtures by false prophets (the secessionists) to get them to believe new doctrines. They have not been deceived.

the one who is in you . . . It is not by means of their own, unaided strength that they are able to resist these false prophets. The source of their power is the Spirit of God who resides in them.

the one who is in the world . . . Satan is the power at work in the world.

v. 5   . . . The false prophets, having been inspired by Satan, are readily heard and accepted by those who are likewise influenced by Satan.

v. 6   . . . In contrast to the "world" which stands in opposition to God, God's truth, and God's people, there is the Church which both believes God's truth and seeks to live it out.

we/us . . . Since John shifts from "you" in verse 4 to "we" in verse 6 it would appear

that here he has in mind not just Christians in general but, specifically, teachers of apostolic doctrine like himself. This is the only unambiguous criterion for truth that John offers: "We are from God and whoever knows God listens to us." Those who follow John and other teachers of apostolic doctrine are following the "Spirit of truth." While it is true the Spirit affirms what is truth for those who know God, the fact is that the secessionists also claim to be led by the Spirit. So this criterion for knowing who is really following God is, by itself, ambiguous. However, the secessionists do not follow John and on this basis are quite clearly outside the bounds of apostolic Christianity.

recognize . . . Those who respond positively to the apostolic preaching are those who are led by the Spirit of truth.

Spirit of truth . . . The reference is probably to the Holy Spirit.

TEXT

STUDY

God's Love and Ours

⁷Dear friends, let us love one another, for love comes from God. Everyone who loves has been born of God and knows God. ⁸Whoever does not love does not know God, because God is love. ⁹This is how God showed his love among us: He sent his one and only Son^a into the world that we might live through him. ¹⁰This is love: not that we loved God, but that he loved us and sent his Son as an atoning sacrifice for^b our sins. ¹¹Dear friends, since God so loved us, we also ought to love one another. ¹²No one has ever seen God; but if we love each other, God lives in us and his love is made complete in us.

¹³We know that we live in him and he in us, because he has given us of his Spirit. ¹⁴And we have seen and testify that the Father has sent his Son to be the Savior of the world. ¹⁵If anyone acknowledges that Jesus is the Son of God, God lives in him and he in God. ¹⁶And so we know and rely on the love God has for us.

God is love. Whoever lives in love lives in God, and God in him. ¹⁷Love is made complete among us so that we will have confidence on the day of judgment, because in this world we are like him. ¹⁸There is no fear in love. But perfect love drives out fear, because fear has to do with punishment. The man who fears is not made perfect in love.

¹⁹We love because he first loved us. ²⁰If anyone says, "I love God," yet hates his brother, he is a liar. For anyone who does not love his brother, whom he has seen, cannot love God, whom he has not seen. ²¹And he has given us this command: Whoever loves God must also love his brother.

Faith in the Son of God

5Everyone who believes that Jesus is the Christ is born of God, and everyone who

READ

First Reading/First Impressions
What are two or three key words or phrases that you see here?
☐ _____ ☐ _____ ☐ _____

Second Reading/Big Idea
In your own words, write what you think is the key verse here.

SEARCH

1. "Love" is mentioned 32 times in this section. What can you learn here about love's:

origin?

connection with
knowing God?

relationship to God's actions?

effects in our lives?

motives?

actions?

perfection?

relationship to fear?

 Continued on next page

2. What do verses 8-15 teach about God? about Christ? about the Holy Spirit?

God, the Father	Jesus Christ	Holy Spirit

3. How is love central to that relationship?

APPLY

Affirmation. Here is a chance to practice a little bit of what this passage is all about. Jot down the names of the people in your group in the left column. Then, in the right column, beside each name, jot down for each person the thing you appreciate most about this person, or the contribution this person has made to your life. For instance: *"John—his encouragement to you. Mary—her warmth and compassion,"* etc.

Then, when you meet as a group, ask one person to sit in silence while the others share what they jotted down about this person. Then take the next person and repeat the process until you have covered everyone in your group. This can get heavy . . . and beautiful.

NAME	THE THING YOU APPRECIATE OR CONTRIBUTION MADE

GROUP AGENDA

Divide into groups of 4 before starting on these questions. Be sure to save plenty of time for affirmation at the close.

TO BEGIN/10 Minutes (Choose 1 or 2)

☐ What characteristic or strength did you get from your father? from your mother? ☐ When you were a child, what chore did you have that was a real burden? ☐ What did you jot down under READ?

TO GO DEEPER/15 Minutes (Choose 2 or 3)

☐ Take time to review your study of "love" in SEARCH question 1. What especially impressed you? bothered you? challenged you? ☐ What did you learn about the Trinity in SEARCH questions 2 and 3? ☐ How does John's message that "God is love" (vv. 8, 16) relate to his message in 1:5 that "God is light"? ☐ From your own experience, how would you explain the verse (5:3), "And his commands are not burdensome."? ☐ Case History: Jim has really tried, but he simply cannot get along with his sixteen-year-old son. Jim is a task-oriented, success-minded driver. He is hard on himself. He is hard on his son. His son, by temperament, is just the opposite. His room is a disaster. His school work is never done on time, and he won't "go out and get a job." Jim is at his wit's end. What can you offer in the way of advice?

Continued on next page

loves the father loves his child as well. ²This is how we know that we love the children of God: by loving God and carrying out his commands. ³This is love for God: to obey his commands. And his commands are not burdensome, ⁴for everyone born of God overcomes the world.

ᵃ9 Or *his only begotten Son*   ᵇ10 Or *as the one who would turn aside his wrath, taking away*

NOTES ON 1 JOHN 4:7-5:4

Summary . . . In 3:23 John stated: "This is his command: to believe in the name of his Son, Jesus Christ, and to love one another as he commanded us." In the previous unit (Unit 8) John expanded on the first part of this command—believing in Jesus. In this unit he expands on the second part of the command—loving other people. John uses the word "love" some 43 times in his epistle. Thirty-two of those uses are in this unit.

v. 7 . . . For the third time John returns to the theme of love. In his first discussion he reminded his readers that love is a command and that to love is to live in the light (2:7-11). In his second discussion he pointed out that Jesus is the model of how to love others and that loving others is evidence that a person belongs to the truth (3:11-20). In this discussion he points out the basis on which he has said all this about love. It is because God himself is love!

GROUP AGENDA
Continued from page 45

TO CLOSE/5 to 20 Minutes (Choose 2 or 3)

☐ Spend most of your time going over the affirmation exercise under APPLY. ☐ Using the "love test" of 5:1 (to love God is to love his children), how are you doing at loving God? Using the test of 5:2-3 (to love others means to obey God's commands), how are you doing at loving others? ☐ Where do you have the greatest trouble loving people—at church, at the office, or at home? ☐ If you could commit yourself to one goal in the next 7 days, what would it be?

love one another . . . John will use this phrase three times in the next five verses (see verses 7, 11, 12). Each time, however, he uses it in a slightly different way. Here he urges his readers to love others because love originates in God.

everyone who loves . . . Since "love comes from God," all acts of love are reflections of God's nature.

v. 8 **whoever does not love does not know God** . . . To claim to be a Christian without living a life of love "is like claiming to be intimate with a foreigner whose language we cannot speak, or to have been born of parents whom we do not in any way resemble" (Stott). Love is the language of God and the mark of his parentage.

God is love . . . This is the second great assertion that John makes in this epistle about the nature of God. (His first assertion is that God is light.) In the first century both these statements about God would have been unexpected. At that time in history there was a deep suspicion that the gods were dark and mysterious and that they cared little about human beings.

vv. 9-10 . . . John now underlines what he said previously, both in his gospel (John 3:16) and in this epistle (1 John 3:16): true love expresses itself in self-sacrificial action undertaken for the benefit of another person without regard to personal cost.

v. 10 . . . Love is initiated by God. Love is his posture toward the human race and this love is given substance by the incarnation of his Son. It is not the other way around. People do not reach out to God with warm feelings or acts of devotion and

thereby trigger his love for them. God is the primal lover. It is his action that draws out their response. Love begins with God.

an atoning sacrifice for our sins . . . By this phrase John describes the saving work that Jesus did on behalf of the human race.

The idea of atonement is tied up with the Old Testament concept of substitution and sacrifice. In the Old Testament, sin was dealt with when a person symbolically placed his sins on an animal that he had brought to the Temple. This animal had to be perfect—without spot or blemish. It was then sacrificed in place of the sinful (imperfect) person. Such substitutionary sacrifices were a picture of what Jesus would one day do once for all men and women.

v. 11 **love one another** . . . This is the second time John uses this phrase. The basis for his exhortation this time is the demonstrated fact that "God so loved us." Jesus' sacrificial death on behalf of the human race assures people that God loves them, and thus releases in them the ability to love others. Because they are loved they can love.

v. 12 **No one has ever seen God** . . . It is not possible for a human being to see God in a direct, unscreened way. Such an encounter is beyond human capability. John reiterates here (and elsewhere) the biblical teaching on this matter (See John 1:18, 5:37; 6:46 as well as Exodus 33:19-23). Perhaps John finds it necessary to say this because some of the secessionists claim to have seen God.

love one another . . . In the third use of this phrase, John states that although God cannot be seen directly, his life can be experienced by people as they love one another. Since God is love, they know him when they love.

vv. 13-16 . . . In these verses John elaborates on the phrase in verse 12: "God lives in us."

vv. 14-16 . . . Christians have the Holy Spirit (v. 13) because they acknowledge that Jesus is the Son of God (vv. 14-15) and because they dwell in his love (v. 16).

vv. 17-21 . . . Having completed his comments on what the statement means that "God lives in us," John next elaborates on a second phrase from verse 12: "his love is made complete in us."

v. 17 confidence . . . Just as believers will have confidence at the Second Coming of Christ (2:28) and as they have confidence when they approach God in prayer (3:19-22), so too they will also have confidence on the day of judgment.

we are like him . . . Once again—as he did in 3:6 and 9—John speaks about a future reality as if it were even now fully realized. In fact, as he has already stated (3:2), believers will not "be like him" until the Second Coming.

v. 18 no fear in love . . . The reason for the confidence believers will have on the day of judgment is that they know God to be their father in whose love they have trusted. People cannot love and fear at the same moment; i.e., it is impossible to approach God with a heart filled both with servile fear and with an overflowing sense of his love for them and their love for him. The love casts out the fear.

fear has to do with punishment . . . This is the root of the fear: they think God is going to punish them. They forget that they are his forgiven children.

v. 19 . . . The love believers exhibit is a response to the prior love of God for them. Love begets love.

v. 20 . . . Love for God is not merely warm inner feelings. Love is not love unless it finds concrete expression via active caring for others. Furthermore, since it is far easier to love a visible person than to love the invisible God, to claim success in the harder task (loving God), while failing in the easier task (loving others) is an absurd and hopeless contradiction.

a liar . . . Three times in this letter John has pointed out lies. It is a lie to claim to follow God and yet live in darkness by not keeping his commands (1:6; 2:4). It is a lie to claim God as Father while denying Jesus his Son (2:22-23). And here he says that it is a lie to claim to love God while hating others. These three lies parallel the three tests of a true Christian. The three lies are the reverse side of the moral, doctrinal and relational tests. The true Christian does not live in an immoral fashion, does not deny Jesus, and does not hate others. Holiness, faith, and love verify the claim to be a child of God.

v. 21 . . . If people truly love God they will keep his commands; and his command is to love others—as John reminds his readers one more time as he ends this lesson on love (see also 2:9-11; 3:10, 23). To love God and to love others is a single inseparable ordinance.

5:1-4a . . . Here John ties together the three tests of faith. "The real link between the three tests is seen to be the new birth. Faith, love and obedience are the natural outgrowth which follows a birth from above" (Stott).

v. 1 believes . . . The tense of the verb (in Greek) indicates that belief is here seen as the *result* of new birth, not its cause. The belief on the part of Christians is clear proof that they have been born of God. However, elsewhere John points to faith as the *condition* of the new birth (John 1:12). The two emphases are complementary: faith enables the new birth to happen and faith is the sign that new birth has taken place.

vv. 2-3 . . . To love God means to keep his commandments and his chief command is to love others (3:23).

v. 2 . . . John states another complementary truth. In 4:20-21 he pointed out that in order to love God one must also love his children. Here he points out that one loves the children of God by loving the Father.

v. 3 burdensome . . . Obedience to the thousands of often picayune rules and regulation promulgated by the scribes and Pharisees was indeed a heavy burden. But obedience to God does not exasperate the Christian since God's laws are of quite a different character (e.g., they are life-giving), and the faith of Christians provides the power for obedience.

UNIT 10—Faith in the Son of God/1 John 5:4-12

TEXT

This is the victory that has overcome the world, even our faith. ⁵Who is it that overcomes the world? Only he who believes that Jesus is the Son of God.

⁶This is the one who came by water and blood—Jesus Christ. He did not come by water only, but by water and blood. And it is the Spirit who testifies, because the Spirit is the truth. ⁷For there are three that testify: ⁸theᵃ Spirit, the water and the blood; and the three are in agreement. ⁹We accept man's testimony, but God's testimony is greater because it is the testimony of God, which he has given about his Son. ¹⁰Anyone who believes in the Son of God has this testimony in his heart. Anyone who does not believe God has made him out to be a liar, because he has not believed the testimony God has given about his Son. ¹¹And this is the testimony: God has given us eternal life, and this life is in his Son. ¹²He who has the Son has life; he who does not have the Son of God does not have life.

ᵃ7, 8 Late manuscripts of the Vulgate *testify in heaven: the Father, the Word and the Holy Spirit, and these three are one.* ⁸*And there are three that testify on earth: the*

STUDY

READ

First Reading/First Impressions
John here reminds me here of a . . . ☐ pastor wrapping up the sermon. ☐ a politician endorsing a candidate for office. ☐ a lawyer making a final appeal to the jury.

Second Reading/Big Idea
What's the main point or topic?

SEARCH

1. Look at the beginning of verse 4 on page 45. From that and verses 4b-5 on this page, what is God's part and our part in "overcoming the world"?

2. from verse 5 plus 2:22-23; 3:23; 4:2, 15; and 5:1, what truths about Jesus must Christians affirm? What is the significance of each?

3. How has God given witness to Jesus by his:

baptism? ("water")—John 1:29-30

death? ("blood")—John 12:23-33

Spirit?—John 14:26; 15:26

4. How do all these confirm that life is found in Jesus?

5. The words "testimony" or "testifies" appears 8 times here. Who is testifying about what to whom? Why?

APPLY

What is one way you feel the new life of Jesus is breaking into your experience?

Scripture memory. 1 John 5:11-12 is probably the best scripture in the Bible on assurance of eternal life for a Christian. If you have not committed these verses to memory, this week would be a good time to do so.

First, to help you think through the meaning, try to rewrite these verses in your own words—your own modern translation.

Then, write out these verses on a 3 × 5 card and place this card on your dashboard or over the kitchen sink, where you can repeat these verses four or five times a day—until you have committed them to memory.

MY PARAPHRASE: 1 John 5:11-12

GROUP AGENDA

Divide into groups of 4 before starting on these questions. Be sure to follow the time recommendations in the agenda.

TO BEGIN/10 Minutes (Choose 1 or 2)

□ Are you more like a turtle or a rabbit? a sprinter or a long distance runner? □ In sports, what was the greatest victory you ever saw? What was the most agonizing defeat? □ What was your favorite hiding place when you were a child? □ Where did you go when a terrible storm was raging outside? □ What did you jot down under READ on your worksheet?

TO GO DEEPER/15 Minutes Choose 2 or 3)

□ Go around your group and share your answers under SEARCH on the worksheet— one person answering question 1, the next person taking question 2, etc. □ What is the difference between believing Jesus and believing in Jesus? □ From what is said here, what do you think the false teachers were teaching about Jesus Christ? □ Case History: Your friend Tom calls himself a "Damascus Road Christian." He sold his business, his big house and his boat. He now gives most of his time to youth work, working with kids in trouble. He thinks everyone should have his experience. How can you deal with this guy?

TO CLOSE/5 to 20 Minutes (Choose 1 or 2)

□ What did you write for APPLY? How did you do on the memorization? □ What are some of the evidences that have led you to believe that life is found in Jesus? □ Where do you struggle in your faith now? □ Has your faith made a difference in your ability to deal with personal tragedy?

NOTES ON 1 JOHN 5:4-12

Summary . . . This is the final unit in the Epistle. (The last few verses will be given over to concluding remarks rather than to extending John's argument.) John has one last statement to make before he concludes his book. It has to do with Jesus. The crucial issue in this whole matter of orthodoxy verses apostasy hinges on one's view of Jesus. If faith is rightly directed at the historic Jesus then (by implication) correct lifestyle and loving relationships will flow from that commitment. But if not—if the Jesus who is honored is more a product of fancy than fact—then quite a different world view will flourish (as the secessionists demonstrate). So John ends where he began—with his testimony to Jesus.

In this final unit, John returns to the themes he struck in his prologue. The parallels between his first and last unit are strong. For example, in the prologue John spoke about testifying: "The life appeared; we have seen it and testify to it . . . (1:2). "Testimony" is also a key theme in this concluding unit. Here John uses the verb "to testify" 4 of the 6 times it appears in the epistle. This is also the only time he uses the noun "testimony" (6 times). In the prologue John also spoke about eternal life: ". . . we proclaim to you the eternal life" (1:2). (The word "life" appeared there 3 times.) So too here in the final unit one finds the concept of eternal life. (The word "life" is used 4 times in 5:4-12).

Furthermore, in the same way that the prologue to the Epistle parallels the prologue to the Gospel (as noted in Unit 1), the final unit of the Epistle parallels the ending of the Gospel of John. In John 20:31 the apostle wrote: "But these are written that you may believe that Jesus is the Christ, the Son of God, and that by believing you may have life in his name." In 5:13—which both sums up this unit and begins his concluding remarks—John states virtually the same thing: "I write these things to you who

believe in the name of the Son of God that you may know that you have eternal life." And indeed, in this unit one finds the same theme with which John concludes the gospel—it is by believing in Jesus as the Son of God that one gains eternal life.

v. 4b victory . . . This word could also be translated "conquering power" or "overcoming power" so as to indicate its close connection in Greek with the verb that follows. Brown translates the beginning of 4b as: "Now this is the conquering power that has conquered the world" (Brown). As John Stott notes: "E. M. Blaiklock, who entitles his devotional studies in this epistle, *Faith is the Victory,* rightly points out the daring of this first-century claim that the victory belongs not to Rome, then reigning supreme, but to Christ and the humble believer in Christ."

overcome the world . . . To the world, God's commands are a burden (5:3); but not to Christians who by virtue of the new birth live in a new sphere. "The spell of the old life has been broken. The fascination of the world has lost its appeal" (Stott). But what is this "conquering power that has conquered the world?" John might have in mind the past victory of Jesus via his death and resurrection (see John 16:33). In this case, Christians would participate in that victory by continuing to win over the world through the power of Jesus. Or John may have in view the conversion or baptism of each believer, which would be the moment he or she entered into the conquering power of Jesus. (The next verses make reference to baptism.) In either case, it is Jesus who has won the victory and Christians who continue to participate in it.

our faith . . . This is the source of the overcoming power of the Christian— confidence and trust that Jesus is the Son of God (see 5:5). It is by means of faith in Jesus that Christians can win over the world which stands in opposition to them as they seek to follow the ways of God.

vv. 6-9 . . . How is it that a person comes to faith in Jesus? By means of reliable witnesses, John answers. In these verses he names three such witnesses that testify to who Jesus is and what he has done. These three witnesses are the water, the blood, and the Holy Spirit.

v. 6 by water and blood . . . By these two phrases John (probably) is referring to Jesus' baptism and Jesus' death. These two events are crucial in understanding who Jesus really is. The secessionists felt that Jesus, the man, became the Christ at his baptism and that the Christ then departed prior to the death of Jesus. In contrast, the apostolic witness (as recorded in the New Testament) asserts that at his baptism, Jesus publicly identified himself with the sins of the people (even though he himself was without sin). And at his death, Jesus died to take away those sins.

Water and blood also function on a secondary level as symbols of purification and redemption. This was their meaning in the rituals described in Leviticus. Furthermore, they would also remind John's readers of the ordinances of baptism and communion (in which water and blood, respectively, are the key elements).

It should be noted, however, that "more ink has been applied to paper in discussing these verses than in discussing any other comparable section of 1 John" (Brown). Plummer calls the phrase "by water and blood" the "most perplexing" in the whole Epistle. It is not clear to the modern reader (as it would have been to the original reader) precisely what John is referring to by this phrase. The notes here, therefore, are on the order of a "best guess"—since other interpretations are possible. For example, some scholars feel that the "water and the blood" refer to the single event of the crucifixion during which "water and blood" flowed from the side of Jesus.

Jesus Christ . . . So as to drive home his point, John uses this dual title which displays the inextricable unity of the divine and human in this one person. He is Jesus of Nazareth and he is the Messiah sent by God. It was Jesus Christ—and not just a human named Jesus—who experienced both baptism and death.

not . . . by water alone . . . The secessionists would agree that the baptism of Jesus was all important. They felt that it was then that the heavenly Christ infused the man Jesus. (In fact, it was the Holy Spirit who descended on Jesus at his baptism.) However, John is insistent that both the baptism and the crucifixion are crucial in understanding Jesus. If it was only a human named Jesus who died on the cross (as John's opponents thought), then universal forgiveness for sin would be impossible. But, in fact, it was Jesus, *the Messiah,* who died on the cross. Furthermore, it would be a lie that God sent his only Son to die for the world (as John states in his gospel in 3:16), if it had been only a human named Jesus who was crucified.

it is the Spirit who testifies . . . John has already stated the fact that there is an inner witness given by the Holy Spirit as to the truth of who Jesus is (see 3:24 & 4:13 as well as 1 Corinthians 12:3). "It is [the Spirit] who deals in our heart the testimony of the water and the blood" (Calvin).

testifies . . . In verses 6-11 John will use the verb "to testify, to bear witness" 4 times and the noun "testimony, witness' 6 times.

the Spirit is the truth . . . The Holy Spirit is the third witness and is qualified to be such because he is, in his essence, truth itself.

v. 7 **three that testify** . . . There are two kinds of testimony: the objective historical witness of the water and the blood (Jesus identified himself with the sins of the people at his baptism and then died for these sins on the cross); and the subjective, experiential witness of the Spirit (Christians experience within themselves the reality and meaning of these events). These two types of witness complement one another. Believers know in their hearts the truthfulness and power of the historical facts of Jesus' life and death.

v. 9 . . . John now clarifies the authority behind these three witnesses. It is God himself. In addition, the object of the three-fold witness is made explicit. It is Jesus his Son. In other words, God bore witness to Jesus in history. At his baptism he declared: "You are my Son, whom I love; with you I am well pleased" (Mark 1:11). In his death, "God presented him as

a sacrifice of atonement through faith in his blood" (Romans 3:25). And God continues to bear witness to Jesus even now via the Holy Spirit who is at work in the hearts of believers.

greater . . . In a law court, testimony is accepted when it is corroborated by two or three witnesses (see Deuteronomy 19:15). How much more substantial is the three-fold testimony of God!

vv. 10-12 . . . Here John points out the result of believing this triple testimony. The believer gains eternal life.

v. 10 . . . The purpose of this testimony is to provoke faith. To accept the testimony is synonymous to believing in Jesus.

believes in . . . It is one thing to *believe* Jesus. It is another to *believe in* Jesus. To believe Jesus means that one accepts what he says as true. To believe in Jesus is to accept who he is. It is to trust him completely and to commit one's life to him.

a liar . . . To reject this triple testimony is to disbelieve God (who is himself the essence of truth). It is to attribute falsehood to him (see 1:10).

v. 11 **eternal life** . . . In receiving the testimony and thus receiving the Son, one also receives eternal life. The Greek word which is here translated "eternal" means "that which belongs to the coming age." But since that age has already broken into the present age, eternal life can be enjoyed even now.

UNIT 11—Concluding Remarks/1 John 5:13-21

TEXT

Concluding Remarks

¹³I write these things to you who believe in the name of the Son of God so that you may know that you have eternal life. ¹⁴This is the assurance we have in approaching God: that if we ask anything according to his will, he hears us. ¹⁵And if we know that he hears us—whatever we ask—we know that we have what we asked of him.

¹⁶If anyone sees his brother commit a sin that does not lead to death, he should pray and God will give him life. I refer to those whose sin does not lead to death. There is a sin that leads to death. I am not saying that he should pray about that. ¹⁷All wrongdoing is sin, and there is sin that does not lead to death.

¹⁸We know that anyone born of God does not continue to sin; the one who was born of God keeps him safe, and the evil one does not touch him. ¹⁹We know that we are children of God, and that the whole world is under the control of the evil one. ²⁰We know also that the Son of God has come and has given us understanding, so that we may know him who is true. And we are in him who is true—even in his Son Jesus Christ. He is the true God and eternal life.

²¹Dear children, keep yourselves from idols.

STUDY

READ

First Reading/First Impressions
In a sentence, express what you see as John's main concern in his conclusion.

Second Reading/Big Idea
In this conclusion, what verse is most important to you? Why?

SEARCH

1. Compare verse 13 with John 20:31. What do these reveal about what is really important to John?

2. How does the awareness that we have God's kind of life affect our prayer life? (v. 14)

3. What does John mean by the condition to this promise? (v. 14)

4. What is the significance of the promises in verses 15-16 to you?

5. In light of Mark 3:22-30 and the false teachers that are plaguing this church, what type of person might John mean by verse 16b?

6. How is the life of the Christian related to the life of Christ in the promises of verse 18?

7. Looking over this passage as a whole, what facts about Jesus does John stress in:

(v. 13)?

(v. 18)?

(v. 20)?

APPLY

What "idol" of the world tempts you away from steadily following Christ today? What can you do practically to "keep yourself" from that idol?

What is one major thing you want to work on as a result of studying this letter?

Prayer. Here's a chance to take God up on his invitation to come to him with your concerns. Take a moment and jot down in the left column three or four things that are concerns to you right now. For instance: *"My family . . . my finances . . . and my future work . .',"* etc. Then, in the right column, for each concern jot down one specific thing you want to ask of God. For instance: *"My Family—closeness and consideration . . .,"* etc.

When you have finished making your "prayer list," spend some time with God talking about these concerns. Then, when you get together with your group, you may want to spend some more time praying together about these concerns.

MY CONCERNS	MY PRAYER REQUESTS

"This is the assurance we have in approaching God: that if we ask anything according to his will, he hears us. And if we know that he hears us—whatever we ask—we know that we have what we asked of him." 1 John 5:14-15

GROUP AGENDA

Divide into groups of 4 before starting on these questions. Be sure to save time at the close for prayer.

TO BEGIN/10 Minutes (Choose 1 or 2)

☐ What came closest to being the "unpardonable sin" in your family when you were growing up: picking your nose in public? playing hooky? chewing tobacco? hogging the bathroom? etc. ☐ Who read to you at night as a child? ☐ Who put you to bed and heard your prayers? ☐ What did you jot down under READ?

TO GO DEEPER/15 Minutes (Choose 2 or 3)

☐ Go around your group and share what you jotted down under SEARCH—one person answering question 1, the next person question 2, etc. ☐ What does it mean to "pray according to his will"? ☐ What is the "sin that leads to death"? Why is the very fear that you have committed "a sin that leads to death" proof that you have done no such thing? ☐ CASE HISTORY: Your two closest friends are not Christian. One says that he was a Christian once, but he would "rather have his fun." The other openly ridicules the Christian faith as a "bunch of myths." How should you pray for these friends?

TO CLOSE/5 to 20 Minutes (Choose 1 or 2)

☐ If you think it would be appropriate, spend the time at the close in "shared prayer," using the list of concerns that you jotted down under APPLY on the worksheet. (Share your concerns first and have each person pray for the person on their right). If this would not be appropriate, use these questions: ☐ What did you write for the first APPLY question? ☐ What do you do when you feel like your prayers are just "bouncing off the ceiling"? ☐ What prayer has God answered recently that you waited on for a long time? ☐ What prayer is still on hold?

NOTES ON 1 JOHN 5:13-21

Summary ... John concludes his epistle with some final comments which relate to the needs of his congregation. Now that his argument against the secessionists is over, John's style changes. he begins to speak more like a pastor than a polemicist. He now speaks directly to the needs of the congregations in Ephesus. In particular, he is anxious that they be encouraged. His encouragement comes in the form of a series of assurances. He begins by assuring them that they do have eternal life since they "believe in the name of the Son of God" (v. 13). He then assures them that God hears and answers prayer (vv. 14-17). Finally, writing in almost a poetic fashion, he assures them that they will be kept safe from a life of habitual sin (v. 18); that they are indeed children of God (v. 19); and that they do, indeed, know the truth (v. 20).

vv. 13-17 ... The previous unit ended with John pointing out that to possess the Son was to possess life and that those who do not possess the Son do not possess life. Just as he has done several times already in this letter when he has described both the positive and the negative side of an issue, he then hastens to reassure his readers that *they* are on the right side and so in no danger. In these verses he assures them that since they believe "in the name of the Son of God" they do, indeed, have eternal life.

v. 13 ... This verse parallels John 20:31 which is the concluding verse of the gospel. (John 21 is an epilogue.) In his gospel John writes: "But these are written that you may believe that Jesus is the Christ, the Son of God, and that by believing you may have life in his name." John wrote his gospel in order to witness to Jesus and so provoke faith in those who did not yet know Christ. By believing in Jesus, they would discover "life." His purpose in the epistle is similar, except that now his words are directed to those who have, in fact, come to believe in Jesus. His purpose is not longer to tell them how to find "life" but, instead, to assure them that they do have eternal life—no matter what the secessionists might say.

these things ... John is referring back to the whole epistle and not just to the previous unit (5:4-12) as comparison with the parallel sentence in the gospel shows. His words there "But these [things] are written that you may believe ..." (John 20:31) are clearly a reference to all he has written in the gospel just as here the phrase "these things" recalls all he has said in the epistle.

eternal life ... The primary meaning of this phrase is not "that which lasts forever" (though this is implied). Rather, what is in view is the very life of God himself which is shared with Christians through Jesus Christ.

vv. 14-17 ... Not only do Christians enjoy the assurance of eternal life, they have a second assurance: that God will answer their prayers.

v. 14 assurance ... Originally this word meant "freedom of speech." It was used to describe the right of all those in a democracy to speak their mind. It later came to mean "confidence" and "boldness." This is the sense in which it is used here in this verse. By this word John refers to the bold confidence that Christians have that they can approach God in prayer and freely speak their minds.

according to his will ... In 3:22 John says that the condition for answered prayer is obedient behavior: we "receive from him [God] anything we ask because we obey his commands and do what pleases him." Here John adds another condition: what we ask must be in accord with God's purposes (see also Matthew 26:39, 42). "Prayer rightly considered is not a device for employing the resources of omnipotence to fulfill our own desires, but a means by which our desires may be redirected according to the mind of God, and made into channels for the forces of his will" (C. H. Dodd).

v. 15 he hears us ... By this phrase John means "he hear us favorably." To know that God hears is to know that "we have what we asked."

we have what we asked ... "Our petitions are granted at once: the results of the granting are perceived in the future" (Plummer).

v. 16 ... John now offers a specific illustration of how prayer operates.

brothers ... John is probably not using this term to refer to other Christians but rather in the broader sense of "neighbors" or possibly even as "nominal church members." This is evident from how he writes about these people. He says that Christians ought to pray that God will give "life" to a "brother" whose sin "does not lead to death." This is not the prayer one prays for Christians who already have eternal life as John has just pointed out in verses 11-12. (This broader use of the word "brother" is also found in 3:16-17 as well as in Matthew 5:22-24 and 7:3-5.)

a sin that leads to death . . . Although John's readers probably understood what he was referring to, it is not at all clear to the modern reader just what this phrase means. However, a few things can be said. For one thing, a specific kind of sin is probably not in view here but rather a lifestyle of habitual, willing, and persistent sinning. Perhaps what John has in mind are people like some of the Pharisees he and the other apostles encountered when they were with Jesus. These men saw Jesus' works and heard his words and yet still pronounced that he was empowered by Satan (Mark 3:22-30). To call good, evil; to understand light to be darkness, is evidence of a mindset that would never call upon God for forgiveness. And if one does not ask, forgiveness cannot be granted. And so one goes to death unrepentant and unforgiven.

I am not saying that he should pray about that . . . While John does not forbid prayer for those involved in a "sin that leads to death," he does not advise it since he doubts its value in such a case.

vv. 18-20 . . . John concludes with a final list of assurances, written in almost poetic style. He names three absolute Christian affirmations by which he summarizes the main themes in the epistle. In verse 18 he focuses on behavior, in verse 19 on relationships, and in verse 20 on belief.

v. 18 . . . The first affirmation relates to Christian behavior.
> It expresses the truth, not that he [the Christian] cannot ever slip into acts of sin, but rather that he does not persist in it habitually. . . . The new birth results in new behaviour. Sin and the child of

God are incompatible. They may occasionally meet; they cannot live together in harmony (Stott).

the one who was born of God . . . By this phrase John refers to Jesus Christ. In the past he has referred to Christians in a similar way (2:29; 3:9; 4:7; 5:1, 4). In other words, almost identical phrases are used to describe both the Christian and the Christ.

keeps him safe . . . The reason that Christians do not abide in sin is that they are kept safe by the power of Jesus Christ who has already destroyed the works of Satan (3:8). (See also John 10:28; 17:12, 15; 1 Peter 1:5; and Jude 24).

v. 19 . . . The second affirmation which John makes is that they are, indeed, "children of God." They are part of the family of God and in relationship with the other children of God. This assertion comes in the form of a categorical statement: either a person is "of God" or a person is of "the world" and as John has already shown, the world is under the control of Satan. John offers no third category. John assures those who are "born of God" (v. 18) that they are "children of God."

v. 20 . . . The third affirmation is that they really do know what is true (over against the secessionists who are promoting a new truth.) John asserts this fact in several ways. First, the source of their insight is "the Son of God" who "has given us understanding." The purpose of this understanding is so that they can know "him who is true." Second, it is not just that in knowing Christ, they accept his teachings to be true. It is deeper than that. They are "in him who is true." Truth is not

something external. They are "in" the truth and the truth is "in them." Furthermore, to be in the Son is to be in the "true God" and share his very life.

has come and has given us understanding . . . By this phrase John highlights the two-fold work of Christ. He came—and thus provided salvation. But he also brought new understanding into the nature of God. Both redemption and revelation are central to the ministry of Jesus.

understanding . . . This is the power or ability to know what is actually so. Specifically, Jesus gave Christians the power to perceive the true God as over against false idols (see v. 21).

v. 21 **keep yourself** . . . This is not the same Greek word that is translated "keep" in verse 18. This word means "guard yourself." So what John is saying is that while Christ keeps the Christian safe (v. 18), so too, simultaneously, the Christians must work at staying away from Satan.

idols . . . These are "God-substitutes" according to Dodd. Whether John has specific idols in mind is not clear. He may mean: "Do not abandon the real for the illusory" (Blaiklock). His imperative may refer either to the false images of the heretical teachers which create a form of idolatry or it may refer to the pagan idols that filled the city of Ephesus. Ephesus was the site of the great temple of Diana which was one of the wonders of the ancient world. It was also the site of immoral rites and the haunt of criminals (because they could not be arrested while in the temple). Its influence permeated the city.

TEXT

¹The elder,

To the chosen lady and her children, whom I love in the truth—and not I only, but also all who know the truth—²because of the truth, which lives in us and will be with us forever:

³Grace, mercy and peace from God the Father and from Jesus Christ, the Father's Son, will be with us in truth and love.

⁴It has given me great joy to find some of your children walking in the truth, just as the Father commanded us. ⁵And now, dear lady, I am not writing you a new command but one we have had from the beginning. I ask that we love one another. ⁶And this is love: that we walk in obedience to his commands. As you have heard from the beginning, his command is that you walk in love. ⁷Many deceivers, who do not acknowledge Jesus Christ as coming in the flesh, have gone out into the world. Any such person is the deceiver and the antichrist. ⁸Watch out that you do not lose what you have worked for, but that you may be rewarded fully. ⁹Anyone who runs ahead and does not continue in the teaching of Christ does not have God; whoever continues in the teaching has both the Father and the Son. ¹⁰If anyone comes to you and does not bring this teaching, do not take him into your house or welcome him. ¹¹Anyone who welcomes him shares in his wicked work.

¹²I have much to write to you, but I do not want to use paper and ink. Instead, I hope to visit you and talk with you face to face, so that our joy may be complete.

¹³The children of your chosen sister send their greetings.

STUDY

READ

First Reading/First Impressions
If I received this letter, I would feel . . , ☐ greatly encouraged. ☐ like I had contributed to a problem John had to straighten out. ☐ like John must have been in a hurry to get this letter out.

Second Reading/Big Idea
What's the main point or topic?

SEARCH

1. Compare verse 1 with verse 13 and 3 John 1. Do you think this letter was sent to a certain woman or generally to a church? Why?

2. What connections do you find between John's themes of ''truth,'' ''love'' and ''obedience'' in verses 1-6?

3. How have the ''deceivers'' (v. 7) lost sight of this connection?

4. In ''running ahead'' of the apostle's teaching, what have they left behind?

5. What potential problems might occur if the church was to offer support and hospitality to these traveling teachers?

APPLY

When it comes to balancing truth and love, on which side do you tend to err? Why?

What guidelines do you use to decide what missionaries or organizations to support?

This would be a good chance to check up on your hospitality motives. Think of the people you have invited over for supper or taken out for supper in the last six months. Jot down their names or initials in the left column. Then, in the right column, jot down who the person is and why you invited this person.

For instance: *Mr. and Mrs. John Smith—old college roommate—strictly social. Bill Ackers— business associate—felt he was lonely after his divorce,* etc.

If you have time, go over the list and code each person with the following symbols in the margin:

□ TBH = To be helpful to someone who is hurting, lonely or in need
□ JFF = Just for fun and a good time
□ DCF = Deep Christian fellowship around Jesus Christ

Analyze your coding to discover what motivates you in offering hospitality.

MY DINNER GUESTS	WHO THEY ARE AND WHY I INVITED THEM

GROUP AGENDA

Divide into groups of 4 before starting on these questions. Try to stick to the time recommendations.

TO BEGIN/10 Minutes (10 Minutes)

□ When you were growing up, where did you gather for family reunions? What was special about these times? Where did you put up guests when they visited your home? □ Whose home do you remember for their warm Christian hospitality? □ Whose home could you drop in on and know you would be welcome—even without calling? □ What did you jot down under READ?

TO GO DEEPER/15 Minutes (Choose 2 or 3)

□ Go around your group and answer the questions under SEARCH—one person taking question 1, the next person question 2, etc. □ What do you think was the situation that caused John to write this letter? □ Why is John so dogmatic about opening your home to false teachers? □ What would be a similar situation today and what do you think John would say about it? □ Case History: Your friend Peter is a wealthy, generous Christian who believes, on the basis of Luke 6:30, that he should give to "whomever the Lord leads to ask me for help since all I have comes from him, and he brings to me those who I can help." What from your experience would you share about evaluating to whom or to what causes you will give financial support?

TO CLOSE/5 to 20 Minutes (Choose 1 or 2)

□ Discuss each of the areas under APPLY. □ Have you ever had to terminate a relationship over some issue related to your faith? What was it? Would you still do so today? □ Since there are so many charlatans in religious clothing, how do you overcome the tendency to just ignore all appeals for money?

NOTES ON 2 JOHN

Summary ... Second and Third John are the shortest letters in the New Testament; so short in fact that virtually everyone concedes that they are genuine. Who would bother to fake such brief, unassuming documents? Their length, incidently, was determined by the size of a standard papyrus sheet (8 × 10 inches). Each letter fits exactly on one sheet.

There is great similarity in style and content between 2 and 3 John. (For example, compare 2 John 1 and 3 John 1; 2 John 4 and 3 John 4; 2 John 12 and 3 John 13-14.) Undoubtedly, both letters were written by the same person. There is also a close connection between 1 John and these two shorter letters (e.g., compare 1 John 4:3 and 2 John 7). All three epistles deal with the same general issues. Therefore, it is highly likely that the "elder" who identifies himself as the author of 2 and 3 John is, indeed, the apostle John who wrote 1 John.

The issue that motivated the writing of 2 and 3 John is that of wandering missionaries. In the days before modern motels; in a time when Roman inns were notorious for being dirty and flea-infested, visiting Christian teachers would turn to the local church for hospitality. The problem was that some of the people seeking room and board were false teachers espousing erroneous doctrines, while others were phonies, pretending to be true prophets but actually only concerned about free hospitality. Even the pagan Greek author Lucian was aware of this kind of abuse of hospitality. In his satirical work *Peregrinus,* he writes about a religious charlatan who lived off the generosity of the church as a way to avoid working. In an attempt to cope with this problem, an early church document called the *Didache,* laid down a series of regulations guiding the reception of itinerant ministers. It said, for example, that true prophets were indeed to be entertained—for a day or two. But if a prophet stayed *three* days this was a sign that he was false. Likewise, if a prophet under the inspiration of the Spirit asks for money, this shows that he is a false prophet.

These are the concerns dealt with in 2 and 3 John. In 2 John, the author discusses false prophets. "Do not welcome such," he says. But in 3 John, he addresses the opposite problem: the failure of Christians to provide hospitality for genuine teachers.

vv. 1-3 ... As was the custom in first-century letters, the writer of this epistle first identifies himself, then he names the recipients of the letter, and concludes his salutation by pronouncing a blessing.

v. 1 **the elder** ... This title appears to be used here in its natural sense (the author is elderly) rather than in its official sense (to designate a leader of the church). John is the last surviving apostle. He is now in his waning years. He is "the Elder," not "an elder." It is not necessary to give his proper name. Everyone knows who he is.

the chosen lady ... It is not clear whether John is addressing an actual person or a church which he personifies by this title. Probably he was referring to a church. This is what Peter did (in 1 Peter 5:13) when he says that "the Elect One in Babylon" (this is the literal translation from the Greek) "sends you her greetings." In this way Peter conveys a message from the church at Rome. "The personification of cities, countries and provinces in female form was a well established convention" (Dodd). It seems unlikely that John had in mind an actual woman because (1) it would be strange that "all who know the truth" would know and love her (v. 1); (2) sometimes she is addressed (in Greek) in the singular (vv. 4, 5, 13) and sometimes in the plural (vv. 6, 8, 10, 12)—the latter being most unlikely were he writing to a particular person; and (3) John's language is much more appropriate for a church than a person (e.g., his statements about love in verses 1, 2, and 5).

vv. 4-11 ... This is the heart of John's message. In verses 4-6 he focuses on the internal life of the local church. He points out its need to walk in truth, obedience, and love. In verses 7-11 he focuses on that external life of the local church, specifically the threat to it posed by false teachers who espouse erroneous doctrine. John makes a sharp distinction between what is true (vv. 4-6) and what is false (vv. 7-11); between Christ and antichrist; and between the commands of God and the deceptions of Satan.

some ... Perhaps John means that while "some" Christians are walking in truth, others are not—in which case his commands are directed to the latter. More likely, he simply means that those from the church whom he has met (or heard about) are walking in truth and he is gladdened by this fact.

commanded us ... Truth is not an option for the Christian. To depart from truth is to disobey God.

vv. 5-6 ... Not only are Christians commanded to believe and obey ("walk in the truth"), they are commanded to love one another.

v. 5 **command** ... If faith were an intuitive leap and love merely a warm feeling, they could not be commanded. But Christian faith is active trust in Christ which shows itself in one's life and Christian love is self-giving service on behalf of others. In other words, neither Christian faith nor Christian love are merely inner emotional responses (though they may involve that). They are outward actions deliberately undertaken by choice.

v. 6 ... Love is expressed in obedience and obedience is shown in love. Thus John points out the reciprocal relationship between love and law. (See John 14:15, 21; 15:10; 1 John 5:2-3; and Matthew 22:37-40.)

vv. 7-11 ... John now turns from true believers to false deceivers. He warns Christians not to be deceived (v. 8). And he tells them not to encourage false teachers by giving them hospitality (vv. 10-11). If his exhortations in verses 4-6 to walk in truth, love, and obedience are followed, the believers will be able to resist the heresy being taught by these false teachers.

v. 7 ... John first defines their error. They have a faulty view of Jesus. They deny the incarnation.

many ... In contrast to "some" children who walk in truth there are the "many" who deceive.

have gone out ... John may be saying that these false teachers were once members of the church but have now left (see 1 John 2:19). Or he may be saying that in the same way that the emissaries of God are sent out into the world, Satan sends out his own emissaries. (Jesus "went out" from the Father into the world [John 7:29; 13:3]. He, in turn, sent out the

disciples into the world [John 17:18; 20:21]).

the deceiver and the antichrist ... These false teachers both deceive people and oppose Christ. Thus they become not just *a* deceiver and *an* antichrist but *the* deceiver and *the* antichrist (1 John 2:18, 22, 26). Jesus also warned his followers about false prophets (Mark 13:5-6, 22).

v. 8 Watch out ... Having stated the problem John then issues his first warning: do not cease in your vigilance.

do not lose ... Failure to be vigilant could result in the loss of reward.

be rewarded fully ... The Greek word translated "rewarded" refers to "the wages of a workman." John's concern is not with the loss of salvation which one does not earn in any case (it is a free gift) but with the loss of due reward for faithful service. However, if people are vigilant, they will gain the wages they have earned.

v. 9 runs ahead ... The Greek word means "to go out in advance." It is used sarcastically here. It is likely that the false teachers were encouraging people to follow their "advanced" views which were based on their "special and superior" insights, in contrast to the "primitive" views of the apostles. John warns his readers that to leave basic Christianity is to run ahead of God!

the teaching of Christ ... By this John refers both to the direct words of Jesus and to the subsequent teaching by the apostles (see Acts 1:1-2; Colossians 3:16; and Hebrews 2:3-4).

does not have God ... The false teachers were claiming that they knew God apart from the teachings of Christ. John asserts that this is not possible (see John 1:18; 14:6-9; 1 John 5:20).

v. 10 ... John now issues his second warning: do not receive or welcome false teachers into your home. This injunction sounds harsh in the light of the New Testament's insistence upon hospitality—including John's own words on the subject (see Romans 12:13; 1 Timothy 3:2; Titus 1:8; Hebrews 13:2; 1 Peter 4:8-10 and 3 John 5-8). However, it is important to notice that John refers to *teachers.* This injunction is not directed at believers who might hold errant views. These false teachers were dangerous because they were like merchants trying to sell a new product (they "bring" into the house the wrong "teaching"). However, John may only be referring here to an "official welcome" by the church and he may mean to deny this only to teachers who deny the incarnation (v. 7).

v. 11 ... Now he gives his reason for the warning: to welcome such a person would encourage an evil work that cuts people off from the Father by denying the Son.

v. 12 much to write ... The Elder has much more to say but he limits himself to one sheet of papyrus, preferring to speak to them in person.

face to face ... In Greek this idiom is literally "mouth to mouth."

v. 13 ... The members of the church from which John writes send greetings.

TEXT

¹The elder,

To my dear friend Gaius, whom I love in the truth.

²Dear friend, I pray that you may enjoy good health and that all may go well with you, even as your soul is getting along well. ³It gave me great joy to have some brothers come and tell about your faithfulness to the truth and how you continue to walk in the truth. ⁴I have no greater joy than to hear that my children are walking in the truth.

⁵Dear friend, you are faithful in what you are doing for the brothers, even though they are strangers to you. ⁶They have told the church about your love. You will do well to send them on their way in a manner worthy of God. ⁷It was for the sake of the Name that they went out, receiving no help from the pagans. ⁸We ought therefore to show hospitality to such men so that we may work together for the truth.

⁹I wrote to the church, but Diotrephes, who loves to be first, will have nothing to do with us. ¹⁰So if I come, I will call attention to what he is doing, gossiping maliciously about us. Not satisfied with that, he refuses to welcome the brothers. He also stops those who want to do so and puts them out of the church.

¹¹Dear friend, do not imitate what is evil but what is good. Anyone who does what is good is from God. Anyone who does what is evil has not seen God. ¹²Demetrius is well spoken of by everyone—and even by the truth itself. We also speak well of him, and you know that our testimony is true.

¹³I have much to write you, but I do not want to do so with pen and ink. ¹⁴I hope to see you soon, and we will talk face to face.

Peace to you. The friends here send their greetings. Greet the friends there by name.

STUDY

READ

First Reading/First Impressions
This letter seems to be basically . . . ☐ a commendation of Gaius. ☐ a condemnation of Diotrephes. ☐ a recommendation for Demetrius.

Second Reading/Big Idea
What do you see as the key sentence in this letter?

SEARCH

1. What conflicts were going on that prompted John to write this letter?

2. In what way does this letter tackle the hospitality issue differently than 2 John?

3. Why would it be so important that these traveling teachers be provided for by the local churches? (vv. 7-8)

4. From the information here and your "sanctified imagination," write a short character sketch of:

Gaius

Diotrephes

Demetrius

5. Specifically, how does Gaius' "love" (v. 6) differ from Diotrephe's "love" (v. 9)?

APPLY

What are some practical ways you can reflect Gaius' desire to help itinerant Christian workers today?

What is one thing you want to change in your life so you might be spoken of as John spoke of Gaius and Demetrius?

Before and After Self Inventory. This being the last session in this course, this would be a good time to stop and take inventory. On the lines below, put two marks to indicate where you are—somewhere between the two extremes:

    x = where I was at the beginning of this course or group
    o = where I am right now

ON KNOWING WHAT I BELIEVE
Completely in the dark _____ The lights have turned on

ON KNOWING WHERE I STAND AND WHY ON ISSUES
Completely in the dark _____ The lights have turned on

ON KNOWING WHAT GOD WANTS ME TO DO WITH MY LIFE
Completely in the dark _____ The lights have turned on

ON KNOWING WHAT GOD WANTS TO DO IN MY CHURCH AND COMMUNITY
Completely in the dark _____ The lights have turned on

GROUP AGENDA

Divide into groups of 4 before starting on these questions. Save time at the close to evaluate your group experience.

TO BEGIN/10 Minutes (Choose 1 or 2)

☐ When you were a kid, who was your idol? Who did you try to imitate? ☐ Did you ever run out of money when you were away from home? What did you do? ☐ Who extended loving hospitality to you when you need it most? ☐ Who deserves the Mother Teresa Award in your community for taking in people who are in need? ☐ What did you jot down under READ on your worksheet?

TO GO DEEPER/15 Minutes (Choose 2 or 3)

☐ Go around your group and share what you jotted down under SEARCH—one person answering questions 1, the next person taking questions 2, etc. ☐ Reading between the lines, what tensions in this early church do you see are still reflected in churches today? ☐ Who are the "they" in verses 6-7? ☐ How would you compare Gaius, Diotrephes and Demetrius? Case History: A friend tells you that an elder in your church told him he ought not to support missionaries who are not connected with the denomination since they are not accountable to the church. Your friend, however, was brought to faith by one of these organizations. What would be your advice in light of 3 John?

TO CLOSE/5 to 20 Minutes (Choose 1 or 2)

☐ This being the last session, spend some time evaluating your experience and deciding what you want to do next. First, share what you jotted down under APPLY on the worksheet. Then, if there is time, here are some questions: ☐ What was the high point in this study for you? ☐ What did you appreciate most about the group you were in? ☐ Would you like to enroll in another course?

61

NOTES ON 3 JOHN

Summary . . . In another short letter, this time addressed to a dear friend, John touches upon the question of itinerant teachers one more time. This time, however, the problem is not with false teachers. The teachers in this letter are true Christians, working "for the sake of the Name" and therefore worthy to receive hospitality. John commends his friend Gaius for opening his home to them even though they were strangers to him. This is the flip side of the issue that was dealt with in 2 John. There John made it quite clear that the church must *not* give hospitality to false teachers. But here he says that it should and must welcome genuine teachers into its midst.

3 John is the shortest letter in the New Testament.

v. 1 **The elder** . . . Both 2 and 3 John were written by the same person, identified only as "the elder." The elder, as it has been argued, is none other than the Apostle John. See the note on 2 John 1.

To my dear friend . . . This is one of only two personal letters in the New Testament. (The other is Philemon.) While certain other letters do bear the name of an individual recipient—for example, Timothy and Titus—they are, in fact, letters meant to be read publicly.

Gaius . . . There are several men by this name mentioned in the New Testament. (See Acts 19:29; 20:4; Romans 16:23; and 1 Corinthians 1:14.) However, "Gaius" was one of the most common names in the Roman Empire. As a result, it is not possible to identify with certainty the Gaius" to whom John writes with any other "Gaius" in the New Testament. What is clear about this particular Gaius is that John had a high and affectionate

regard for him; that he freely offered Christian hospitality to others; and that he was a leader in the local church.

whom I love in the truth . . . Truth is the sphere in which love flourishes. See 2 John 1-6.

v. 2 . . . It was not uncommon for Greek letters to begin with a wish that the recipient would enjoy good health.

all may go well . . . The single Greek word which is translated by this phrase means, literally, "have a good journey." It eventually came to mean "prosper" or "succeed."

even as your soul is getting along well . . . This is, literally, "as your soul prospers." John desires spiritual as well as physical well-being for his friend.

v. 3 . . . John knows that Gaius' "soul" is "getting along well" (as he says in verse 2) because of the news he received about him from "some brothers" who had visited him.

faithfulness to the truth . . . This was one of several characteristics of Gaius that John singles out for commendation. As John said over and over again in his first epistle, it is important that Christians adhere to the truth of the gospel. Gaius had done just this. In verse 6, John will point out a second characteristic of Gaius: he loved others. This is another trait that is characteristic of the true Christian as defined by John in his first epistle. Gaius' life was a living demonstration of the "truth in love" that John speaks of in 1 John 3:18 and 2 John 1-6.

v. 4 **my children** . . . Paul used this phrase to describe those who conversion to Christ he assisted. Perhaps, therefore, Gaius is John's spiritual son.

walking in the truth . . . Gaius did not just *know* the truth, he *did* it. He lived what he believed. He let his theological convictions guide his moral behavior.

vv. 5-8 . . . Here John commends Gaius for showing hospitality to the visiting teachers. John's words in verses 5-8 stand in sharp contrast to what he wrote in 2 John 10-11 where he warned *against* offering hospitality to certain teachers. The difference, of course, is that in 2 John he was concerned about false teachers and here he discusses "brothers" who went out "for the sake of the Name" and who "work . . . for the truth." 2 and 3 John must be read together to get a balanced picture of the situation in the early church when it came to itinerant teachers.

vv. 5-6 . . . Having commended Gaius for "walking in the truth," John now points to a concrete example of what this actually involves. Gaius opened his house to some fellow Christians even though he did not know them. This is love in action. These visiting Christian teachers, at some later date, spoke appreciatively to John about the hospitality Gaius showed them.

v. 5 **strangers** . . . What pleases John especially is that Gaius opened his home to those he did not know personally.

v. 6 **send them on their way in a manner worthy of God** . . . Not only did he host these visitors while they were in town, but he provided them with provisions (probably food and money) to be used on the next leg of the journey. The verb used here, which means literally "to send forward," came to refer in this context to providing missionaries with supplies for their onward journey (see Acts 15:3; Romans 15:24; 1 Corinthians 16:6, 11; 2 Corinthians 1:16; and Titus 3:13).

v. 7 **The Name** ... Jesus Christ.

they went out ... This term was used to describe setting out on a mission for Christ. In other words, these visitors were not ordinary travelers but Christian missionaries.

receiving no help from the pagans ... John is not saying that they could not accept gifts from pagans but that as a matter of policy they did not do so— unlike many of the itinerant nonChristian teachers of that era. "Devotees of various religions tramped the roads, extolling the virtues of the deity of their choice and collecting subscriptions from the deity of their choice and collecting subscriptions from the public" (C. H. Dodd).

v. 8 ... "If the first reason for entertaining traveling missionaries is that they are brethren whom we should honor for setting out for the sake of the Name, the second is the much more practical one that they have no other means of support" (Stott).

hospitality ... The ancient world saw hospitality as almost a sacred duty. For example, there was in operation at that time a system of "guest friendships" whereby families agreed to look after each other's members as they travelled through their community. Such hospitality was claimed by presenting a "token" that identified the traveller.

vv. 9-10 ... John sets in contrast to the hospitality of Gaius the hostility of Diotrephes

v. 9 **Diotrephes** ... He and Gaius may have been members of the same congregation or, more likely, of neighboring congregations. In any case, they act in opposite ways when it comes to hospitality. Gaius welcomes visiting teachers. Diotrephes refuses to receive them. This may have to do with his desire "to be first." Visiting teachers would be a threat to his preeminence.

loves to be first ... Personal aggrandizement was what Diotrephes craved.

v. 10 ... John here identifies three aspects of Diotrephes' behavior which is not in accord with the gospel.

I will call attention ... John may be forced to deal with this challenge to his apostolic authority.

gossiping maliciously ... The first thing Diotrephes did was to attempt to undermine John's authority by "talking nonsense" about him—which is what this phrase means literally.

refuses to welcome ... Secondly, he defies John's instructions and refuses to offer hospitality to Christian brothers.

puts them out of the church ... Third, he is not content simply to "refuse to welcome" these missionaries, he prevents others from offering hospitality by threatening excommunication.

v. 11 **imitate** ... John warns Gaius not to model his behavior after that of Diotrephes. Instead, he should copy a good example.

Anyone who does what is good is from God.... Behavior is indicative of a relationship with God—or, as John goes on to say, the lack of a relationship with God.

v. 12 ... John names yet another first-century Christian leader: Demetrius. He gives a three-fold testimony to his character. He is well regarded by all who know him. His Christian character is self-evident. And he is highly regarded by John himself.

Demetrius ... Demetrius probably delivered this letter to Gaius. Since he was unknown to Gaius, John writes this three-way recommendation. Demetrius may himself have been a wandering missionary whom John wishes the house-church to receive. Two other men by the name of Demetrius are mentioned in the New Testament: the silversmith in Ephesus (Acts 19:23-27) and a friend of Paul (Colossians 4:14; 2 Timothy 4:10 and Philemon 24—Demas is short for Demetrius). In an ancient document it says that John appointed the Demetrius mentioned here to be Bishop of Philadelphia.

vv. 13-14 ... These verses are virtually identical to 2 John 12. See the notes for that verse.

ACKNOWLEDGEMENTS

In preparing notes such as these, there is a strong dependence upon the tools of New Testament research (e.g., Arndt and Gingrich Greek-English Lexicon; Bible Dictionaries; New Testament Introductions; etc.). In addition, use has been made of various commentaries. While it is not possible as one would desire, given the scope and aim of this book, to acknowledge in detail the input of each author, the source of direct quotes and special insights is given. The three key commentaries that were used are: Raymond E. Brown, *The Epistles of John* (The Anchor Bible), Garden City, NY: Doubleday and Company, Inc., 1982; I. Howard Marshall, *The Epistles of John* (The New International Commentary on the New Testament), Grand Rapids: Wm. B. Eerdmans Publishing Co., 1978; and John R. W. Stott, *The Epistles of John* (Tyndale New Testament Commentaries), London: The Tyndale Press, 1964.

In addition, reference was made to William Barclay, *The Letters of John and Jude* (The Daily Study Bible), Edinburgh: The Saint Andrew Press, 1958; F. F. Bruce, *The Epistle of John,* Grand Rapids: Wm. B. Eerdmans Publishing Co., 1970; C. H. Dodd, *The Johannine Epistles* (MNTC), London: Hodder and Stoughton, 1946; Hass, deJonge, Swellongrebel, *A Translator's Handbook on the Letters of John,* London: United Bible Societies, 1972; J. L. Houlden, *A Commentary on the Johannine Epistles* (Harper's New Testament Commentaries), New York: Harper & Row, 1973; Marilyn Kunz and Catherine Schell, *1 John and James* Neighborhood Bible Studies), Wheaton: Tyndale House Publishers, 1965; and Rodney A. Whitacre, *Johannine Polemic: The Role of Tradition and Theology* (SBL Dissertation Series 67), Chico, CA: Scholars Press, 1982.

Special thanks go to Marcus Grodi who prepared a set of questions and notes for use in drafting the original manuscript; and to Barbara Denike who typed the first version of this study and to Tina Howard who assisted in the preparation of the final version. Dr. Rodney Whitacre served as technical consultant on this project and contributed a number of fine insights into the Johannine materials.

Copyright Endorsements